FOREIGN AFFAIRS

Special Collection

Foreign Affairs Special Collection: Best of 2014

Editor Gideon Rose Introduces the Collection

We've published a ton of great content in 2014, and we've picked out ten of our favorite articles from the print edition and ten from the web to show you just what we've been up to over the last year. We hope you enjoy the collection and come back for more in 2015.

ON INEQUALITY:
In "Capital Punishment," Tyler Cohen explains why French economist Thomas Piketty's book on economic inequality is brilliant but fundamentally flawed.

ON UKRAINE:
"Why the Ukraine Crisis Is the West's Fault," John Mearsheimer's blockbuster article on Washington and its European allies' responsibility for the Ukraine crisis, will make you rethink your opinion of recent Russian behavior.

ON PAKISTAN'S FEMALE SOLDIERS:
In "Meet Pakistan's Lady Cadets," Aeyliya Husain offers an eye-opening account of a small group of women making their way through the Pakistan Military Academy.

ON TUNNELS:
Hamas is only the latest in a long line of groups to use tunnels to wage war. In "Notes from the Underground," Arthur Herman writes that there's no way to know how long drones and the like will last. But as long as there is warfare, tunnels will almost certainly be part of the fight

Visit ForeignAffairs.com for more on these topics—and all our other great content.

Capital Punishment

Why a Global Tax on Wealth Won't End Inequality

Tyler Cowen FROM OUR MAY/JUNE 2014 ISSUE

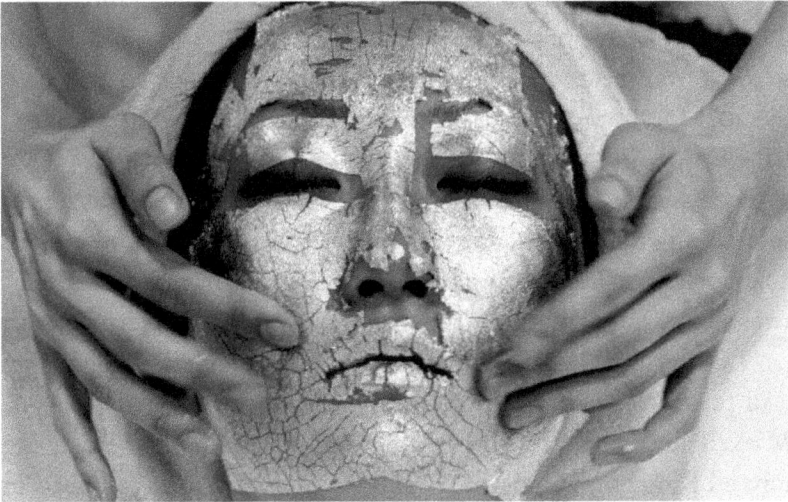

A model gets a 24-carat gold leaf facial at the Beautyworld Japan 2007 trade fair in Tokyo, May 7, 2007. (Toru Hanai / Courtesy Reuters)

Capital in the Twenty-first Century. BY THOMAS PIKETTY. TRANSLATED BY ARTHUR GOLDHAMMER. Belknap Press, 2014, 696 pp. $39.95.

Every now and then, the field of economics produces an important book; this is one of them. Thomas Piketty's tome will put capitalist wealth back at the center of public debate, resurrect interest in the subject of wealth distribution, and revolutionize how people view the history of income inequality. On top of that, although the book's prose (translated from the original French) might not

1

qualify as scintillating, any educated person will be able to understand it—which sets the book apart from the vast majority of works by high-level economic theorists.

Piketty is best known for his collaborations during the past decade with his fellow French economist Emmanuel Saez, in which they used historical census data and archival tax records to demonstrate that present levels of income inequality in the United States resemble those of the era before World War II. Their revelations concerning the wealth concentrated among the richest one percent of Americans—and, perhaps even more striking, among the richest 0.1 percent—have provided statistical and intellectual ammunition to the left in recent years, especially during the debates sparked by the 2011 Occupy Wall Street protests and the 2012 U.S. presidential election.

In this book, Piketty keeps his focus on inequality but attempts something grander than a mere diagnosis of capitalism's ill effects. The book presents a general theory of capitalism intended to answer a basic but profoundly important question. As Piketty puts it: "Do the dynamics of private capital accumulation inevitably lead to the concentration of wealth in ever fewer hands, as Karl Marx believed in the nineteenth century? Or do the balancing forces of growth, competition, and technological progress lead in later stages of development to reduced inequality and greater harmony among the classes, as Simon Kuznets thought in the twentieth century?"

Although he stops short of embracing Marx's baleful vision, Piketty ultimately lands on the pessimistic end of the spectrum. He believes that in capitalist systems, powerful forces can push at various times toward either equality or inequality and that, therefore, "one should be wary of any economic determinism." But in the end, he concludes that, contrary to the arguments of Kuznets and other mainstream thinkers, "there is no natural, spontaneous process to prevent destabilizing, inegalitarian forces from prevailing permanently." To forestall such an outcome, Piketty proposes, among other things, a far-fetched plan for the global taxation of wealth—a call to radically redistribute the fruits of capitalism to ensure the system's survival. This is an unsatisfying conclusion to a groundbreaking work of analysis that is frequently brilliant—but flawed, as well.

THE RICH ARE DIFFERENT

Piketty derives much of his analysis from a close examination of an important but generally overlooked driver of economic inequality: in contemporary market economies, the rate of return on investment frequently outstrips the overall growth rate, an imbalance that Piketty renders as r > g. Thanks to the effect of compounding, if that discrepancy persists over time, the wealth held by capitalists increases far more rapidly than other kinds of earnings, eventually outstripping them by a wide margin. To measure this effect, Piketty focuses on the annual capital-to-income ratio, which expresses the size of a country's total stock of wealth relative to the income generated by its economy in a single year. Capital wealth is generally much larger than yearly national income—in the case of today's developed economies, about five to six times as large.

Piketty expertly narrates the story of how that gap has played a major role in economic history since the dawn of the modern era. The peace and relative stability enjoyed by western Europe during the second half of the nineteenth century allowed for enormous capital accumulation. Unprecedented concentrations of wealth arose, boosting inequality. But two world wars and the Great Depression destroyed capital and interrupted that trend. Those cataclysms led to a new, more egalitarian era, shaped by postwar rebuilding, a strong demand for labor, rapidly growing populations, and technological innovation. The three decades between 1950 and 1980 were truly unusual; the constellation of economic and demographic variables that produced prosperity during that period will probably not be re-created anytime soon.

After 1980, ongoing capital accumulation, slower technological progress, and rising inequality heralded a regression to something akin to the conditions of the nineteenth century. But few notice the resemblance between now and then, especially in one crucial respect: the role of inherited wealth. So many nineteenth-century novelists were obsessed with estates and inheritance—think of Jane Austen, George Eliot, or Charles Dickens—precisely because receiving wealth from one's parents was such a common way of prospering during that era. In nineteenth-century France, the flow of inheritances represented about 20–25 percent of national income during a typical year. According to Piketty's calculations, the Western world is headed toward a roughly comparable situation. The relatively thrifty and wealthy baby boomers will soon begin to die off in greater numbers, and inheritance as a source of income disproportionately benefits the families of the very wealthy.

At the core of Piketty's story are the tragic consequences of capitalism's success: peace and a declining population bring notable gains, but they also create a society dominated by wealth and by income from capital. In essence, Piketty presents a novel and somewhat disconcerting way of thinking about how hard it is to avoid growing inequality.

Yet there are flaws in this tale. Although r > g is an elegant and compelling explanation for the persistence and growth of inequality, Piketty is not completely clear on what he means by the rate of return on capital. As Piketty readily admits, there is no single rate of return that everyone enjoys. Sitting on short-term U.S. Treasury bills does not yield much: a bit over one percent historically in inflation-adjusted terms and, at the moment, negative real returns. Equity investments such as stocks, on the other hand, have a historical rate of return of about seven percent. In other words, it is risk taking—a concept mostly missing from this book—that pays off.

That fact complicates Piketty's argument. Piketty estimates that the general annual rate of return on capital has averaged between four and five percent (pretax) and is unlikely to deviate too far from this range. But in too many parts of his argument, he seems to assume that investors can reap such returns automatically, with the mere passage of time, rather than as the result of strategic risk taking. A more accurate picture of the rate of return would incorporate risk and take into account the fact that although the stock of capital typically grows each year, sudden reversals and retrenchments are inevitable. Piketty repeatedly serves up the appropriate qualifications and caveats about his model, but his analysis and policy recommendations nevertheless reflect a notion of capital as a growing, homogeneous blob which, at least under peaceful conditions, ends up overshadowing other economic variables.

Furthermore, even if one overlooks Piketty's hazy definition of the rate of return, it is difficult to share his confidence that the rate, however one defines it, is likely to be higher than the growth rate of the economy. Normally, economists think of the rate of return on capital as diminishing as investors accumulate more capital, since the most profitable investment opportunities are taken first. But in Piketty's model, lucrative overseas investments and the growing financial sophistication of the superwealthy keep capital returns permanently high. The more prosaic reality is that most capital stays in its home country and also has a hard time beating randomly selected stocks. For those reasons, the future of capital income looks far less glamorous than Piketty argues.

RICARDO REDUX

Piketty, in a way, has updated the work of the British economist David Ricardo, who, in the early nineteenth century, identified the power of what he termed "rent," which he defined as the income earned from taking advantage of the difference in value between more and less productive lands. In Ricardo's model, rent—the one kind of income that did not suffer from diminishing returns—swallowed up almost everything else, which is why Ricardo feared that landlords would come to dominate the economy.

Of course, since Ricardo's time, the relative economic importance of land has plummeted, and his fear now seems misplaced. During the twentieth century, other economists, such as Friedrich Hayek and the other thinkers who belonged to the so-called Austrian School, understood that it is almost impossible to predict which factors of production will provide the most robust returns, since future economic outcomes will depend on the dynamic and essentially un-foreseeable opportunities created by future entrepreneurs. In this sense, Piketty is like a modern-day Ricardo, betting too much on the significance of one asset in the long run: namely, the kind of sophis-ticated equity capital that the wealthy happen to hold today.

Piketty's concern about inherited wealth also seems misplaced. Far from creating a stagnant class of rentiers, growing capital wealth has allowed for the fairly dynamic circulation of financial elites. Today, the Rockefeller, Carnegie, and Ford family fortunes are quite dispersed, and the benefactors of those estates hardly run the United States, or even rival Bill Gates or Warren Buffett in the financial rankings. Gates' heirs will probably inherit billions, but in all likelihood, their fortunes will also be surpassed by those of fu-ture innovators and tycoons, most of whom will not come from millionaire families.

To be sure, outside the realm of the ultra-elites, the United States suffers from unfairness in terms of who gets ahead in life, and a lack of upward mobility profoundly affects the prospects of lower-income Americans. Still, the success of certain immigrant groups suggests that cultural factors play a more significant role in mobility than does the capital-to-income ratio, since the children and grandchildren of immigrants from those groups tend to ad-vance socioeconomically even if their forebears arrived without much in the way of accumulated fortunes.

It is also worth noting that many wealth accumulators never fully diversify their holdings, or even come close to doing so. Gates, for example, still owns a lot of Microsoft stock—perhaps out of a desire for control, or because of a sentimental attachment to the company he co-founded, or maybe just due to excessive optimism. Whatever the reasons, over time such concentrations of financial interest hasten the circulation of elites by making it possible for the wealthy to suffer large losses very rapidly.

And in the end, even the most successful companies will some-day fall, and the fortunes associated with them will dissipate. In the very long run, the most significant gains will be reaped by institutions that are forward-looking and rational enough to fully diversify. As Piketty discusses, that category includes the major private U.S. universities, and indeed the list of the top schools has not changed much over many decades. Harvard and other elite universities might, in fact, emerge as the true rentiers of the contemporary era: as of 2008, the top 800 U.S. colleges and universities controlled almost $400 billion in assets.

DOING WELL, THEN DOING GOOD

Piketty fears the stasis and sluggishness of the rentier, but what might appear to be static blocks of wealth have done a great deal to boost dynamic productivity. Piketty's own book was published by the Belknap Press imprint of Harvard University Press, which received its initial funding in the form of a 1949 bequest from Waldron Phoenix Belknap, Jr., an architect and art historian who inherited a good deal of money from his father, a vice president of Bankers Trust. (The imprint's funds were later supplemented by a grant from Belknap's mother.) And consider Piketty's native France, where the scores of artists who relied on bequests or family support to further their careers included painters such as Corot, Delacroix, Courbet, Manet, Degas, Cézanne, Monet, and Toulouse-Lautrec and writers such as Baudelaire, Flaubert, Verlaine, and Proust, among others.

Notice, too, how many of those names hail from the nineteenth century. Piketty is sympathetically attached to a relatively low capital-to-income ratio. But the nineteenth century, with its high capital-to-income ratios, was in fact one of the most dynamic periods of European history. Stocks of wealth stimulated invention by liberating creators from the immediate demands of the marketplace and allowing them to explore their fancies, enriching generations to come.

Piketty's focus on the capital-to-income ratio is novel and worthwhile. But his book does not convincingly establish that the ratio is important or revealing enough to serve as the key to understanding significant social change. If wealth keeps on rising relative to income, but wages also go up, most people will be happy. Of course, in the past few decades, median wages have been stagnant in many developed countries, including the United States. But the real issue, then, is wages—not wealth. A high capital-to-income ratio might be one factor depressing wages, but it hardly seems central—and Piketty does not claim, much less show, that it is.

Two other factors have proved much more important: technological changes during the past few decades that have created a globalized labor market that rewards those with technical knowledge and computer skills and competition for low-skilled jobs from labor forces overseas, especially China. Piketty discusses both of those issues, but he puts them to the side rather than front and center.

Of course, income and wealth inequalities have risen in most of the world's developed nations, and those processes will likely continue and perhaps intensify in the immediate future. But for the world as a whole, economic inequalities have been falling for several decades, mostly thanks to the economic rise of China and India. Growth in those countries has depended in part on policies of economic liberalization, which themselves were inspired and enabled, to a certain extent, by capital accumulation in the West. The relative global peace of the postwar period might have bred inequality in rich countries, but it has also led to reform and economic opportunity in poorer countries. It is no accident that communism was the product of war and civil conflict.

TAXMAN

The final chapters of the book, which contain Piketty's policy recommendations, are more ideological than analytic. In these sections, Piketty's preconceptions lead to some untenable conclusions. His main proposal is a comprehensive international agreement to establish a progressive tax on individual wealth, defined to include every kind of asset. Piketty concedes that this is a "utopian idea" but also insists that it is the best possible solution to the problem. He hedges a bit on the precise numbers but suggests that wealth below 200,000 euros be taxed at a rate of 0.1 percent, wealth between 200,000 and one million euros at 0.5 percent, wealth between one million and five million euros at 1.0 percent, and wealth above five million euros at 2.0 percent.

Although he recognizes the obvious political infeasibility of such a plan, Piketty has nothing to say about the practical difficulties, distorting effects, and potential for abuse that would inevitably accompany such intense government control of the economy. He points to estimates he has previously published in academic papers as evidence that such a confiscatory regime would not harm the labor supply in the short term. But he neglects the fact that in the long run, taxes of that level would surely lower investments in human capital and the creation of new businesses. Nor does he recognize one crucial implication of his own argument about the power of nondiminishing capital returns: if capital is so mobile and dynamic that it can avoid diminishing returns, as Piketty claims, then it will probably also avoid being taxed, which means that the search for tax revenue will have to shift elsewhere, and governments will find that soaking the rich does not really work.

Piketty also ignores other problems that would surely stem from so much wealth redistribution and political control of the economy, and the book suffers from Piketty's disconnection from practical politics—a condition that might not hinder his standing in the left-wing intellectual circles of Paris but that seems naive when confronted with broader global economic and political realities. In perhaps the most revealing line of the book, the 42-year-old Piketty writes that since the age of 25, he has not left Paris, "except for a few brief trips." Maybe it is that lack of exposure to conditions and politics elsewhere that allows Piketty to write the following words with a straight face: "Before we can learn to efficiently organize public financing equivalent to two-thirds to three-quarters of national income"—which would be the practical effect of his tax plan—"it would be good to improve the organization and operation of the existing public sector." It would indeed. But Piketty makes such a massive reform project sound like a mere engineering problem, comparable to setting up a public register of vaccinated children or expanding the dog catcher's office.

Worse, Piketty fails to grapple with the actual history of the kind of wealth tax he supports, a subject that has been studied in great detail by the economist Barry Eichengreen, among others. Historically, such taxes have been implemented slowly, with a high level of political opposition, and with only modestly successful results in terms of generating revenue, since potentially taxable resources are often stashed in offshore havens or disguised in shell companies and trusts. And when governments have imposed significant wealth taxes quickly—as opposed to, say, the slow evolution of local, consent-based property taxes—those policies have been accompanied by crumbling economies and political instability.

Recent wealth-tax regimes in the European Union offer no exceptions to this general rule. In 2011, Italy introduced a wealth tax on real estate, but Rome retracted the plan after the incumbent government was dealt a major blow in elections last year, partly owing to public dissatisfaction with the tax scheme. Last year, the government of the Republic of Cyprus imposed the equivalent of a tax on bank deposits, only to see the tax contribute to, rather than reverse, the island's economic struggles.

The simple fact is that large wealth taxes do not mesh well with the norms and practices required by a successful and prosperous capitalist democracy. It is hard to find well-functioning societies based on anything other than strong legal, political, and institutional respect and support for their most successful citizens. Therein lies the most fundamental problem with Piketty's policy proposals: the best parts of his book argue that, left unchecked, capital and capitalists inevitably accrue too much power—and yet Piketty seems to believe that governments and politicians are somehow exempt from the same dynamic.

A more sensible and practicable policy agenda for reducing inequality would include calls for establishing more sovereign wealth funds, which Piketty discusses but does not embrace; for limiting the tax deductions that noncharitable nonprofits can claim; for deregulating urban development and loosening zoning laws, which would encourage more housing construction and make it easier and cheaper to live in cities such as San Francisco and, yes, Paris; for offering more opportunity grants for young people; and for improving education. Creating more value in an economy would do more than wealth redistribution to combat the harmful effects of inequality.

TYLER COWEN is Professor of Economics at George Mason University and writes for the blog Marginal Revolution. Follow him on Twitter @tylercowen.

The Return of Geopolitics

The Revenge of the Revisionist Powers

Walter Russell Mead   FROM OUR MAY/JUNE 2014 ISSUE

Russian servicemen in historical uniforms take part in a military parade in Moscow's Red Square, November 3, 2011. (Denis Sinyakov / Courtesy Reuters)

So far, the year 2014 has been a tumultuous one, as geopolitical rivalries have stormed back to center stage. Whether it is Russian forces seizing Crimea, China making aggressive claims in its coastal waters, Japan responding with an increasingly assertive strategy of its own, or Iran trying to use its alliances with Syria and Hezbollah to dominate the Middle East, old-fashioned power plays are back in international relations.

The United States and the EU, at least, find such trends disturbing. Both would rather move past geopolitical questions of territory and military power and focus instead on ones of world order and global governance: trade liberalization, nuclear nonproliferation, human rights, the rule of law, climate change, and so on. Indeed, since the end of the Cold War, the most important objective of U.S. and EU foreign policy has been to shift international relations away from zero-sum issues toward win-win ones. To be dragged back into old-school contests such as that in Ukraine doesn't just divert time and energy away from those important questions; it also changes the character of international politics. As the atmosphere turns dark, the task of promoting and maintaining world order grows more daunting.

But Westerners should never have expected old-fashioned geopolitics to go away. They did so only because they fundamentally misread what the collapse of the Soviet Union meant: the ideological triumph of liberal capitalist democracy over communism, not the obsolescence of hard power. China, Iran, and Russia never bought into the geopolitical settlement that followed the Cold War, and they are making increasingly forceful attempts to overturn it. That process will not be peaceful, and whether or not the revisionists succeed, their efforts have already shaken the balance of power and changed the dynamics of international politics.

A FALSE SENSE OF SECURITY

When the Cold War ended, many Americans and Europeans seemed to think that the most vexing geopolitical questions had largely been settled. With the exception of a handful of relatively minor problems, such as the woes of the former Yugoslavia and the Israeli-Palestinian dispute, the biggest issues in world politics, they assumed, would no longer concern boundaries, military bases, national self-determination, or spheres of influence.

One can't blame people for hoping. The West's approach to the realities of the post–Cold War world has made a great deal of sense, and it is hard to see how world peace can ever be achieved without replacing geopolitical competition with the construction of a liberal world order. Still, Westerners often forget that this project rests on the particular geopolitical foundations laid in the early 1990s.

In Europe, the post–Cold War settlement involved the unification of Germany, the dismemberment of the Soviet Union, and the integration of the former Warsaw Pact states and the Baltic republics into NATO and the EU. In the Middle East, it entailed the dominance of Sunni powers that were allied with the United States (Saudi Arabia, its Gulf allies, Egypt, and Turkey) and the double containment of Iran and Iraq. In Asia, it meant the uncontested dominance of the United States, embedded in a series of security relationships with Japan, South Korea, Australia, Indonesia, and other allies.

This settlement reflected the power realities of the day, and it was only as stable as the relationships that held it up. Unfortunately, many observers conflated the temporary geopolitical conditions of the post–Cold War world with the presumably more final outcome of the ideological struggle between liberal democracy and Soviet communism. The political scientist Francis Fukuyama's famous formulation that the end of the Cold War meant "the end of history" was a statement about ideology. But for many people, the collapse of the Soviet Union didn't just mean that humanity's ideological struggle was over for good; they thought geopolitics itself had also come to a permanent end.

At first glance, this conclusion looks like an extrapolation of Fukuyama's argument rather than a distortion of it. After all, the idea of the end of history has rested on the geopolitical consequences of ideological struggles ever since the German philosopher Georg Wilhelm Friedrich Hegel first expressed it at the beginning of the nineteenth century. For Hegel, it was the Battle of Jena, in 1806, that rang the curtain down on the war of ideas. In Hegel's eyes, Napoleon Bonaparte's utter destruction of the Prussian army in that brief campaign represented the triumph of the French Revolution over the best army that prerevolutionary Europe could produce. This spelled an end to history, Hegel argued, because in the future, only states that adopted the principles and techniques of revolutionary France would be able to compete and survive.

Adapted to the post–Cold War world, this argument was taken to mean that in the future, states would have to adopt the principles of liberal capitalism to keep up. Closed, communist societies, such as the Soviet Union, had shown themselves to be too uncreative and unproductive to compete economically and militarily with liberal states. Their political regimes were also shaky, since no social form other than liberal democracy provided enough freedom and dignity for a contemporary society to remain stable.

To fight the West successfully, you would have to become like the West, and if that happened, you would become the kind of wishy-washy, pacifistic milquetoast society that didn't want to fight about anything at all. The only remaining dangers to world peace would come from rogue states such as North Korea, and although such countries might have the will to challenge the West, they would be too crippled by their obsolete political and social structures to rise above the nuisance level (unless they developed nuclear weapons, of course). And thus former communist states, such as Russia, faced a choice. They could jump on the modernization bandwagon and become liberal, open, and pacifistic, or they could cling bitterly to their guns and their culture as the world passed them by.

At first, it all seemed to work. With history over, the focus shifted from geopolitics to development economics and nonproliferation, and the bulk of foreign policy came to center on questions such as climate change and trade. The conflation of the end of geopolitics and the end of history offered an especially enticing prospect to the United States: the idea that the country could start putting less into the international system and taking out more. It could shrink its defense spending, cut the State Department's appropriations, lower its profile in foreign hotspots—and the world would just go on becoming more prosperous and more free.

This vision appealed to both liberals and conservatives in the United States. The administration of President Bill Clinton, for example, cut both the Defense Department's and the State Department's budgets and was barely able to persuade Congress to keep paying U.S. dues to the UN. At the same time, policymakers assumed that the international system would become stronger and wider-reaching while continuing to be conducive to U.S. interests. Republican neo-isolationists, such as former Representative Ron Paul of Texas, argued that given the absence of serious geopolitical challenges, the United States could dramatically cut both military spending and foreign aid while continuing to benefit from the global economic system.

After 9/11, President George W. Bush based his foreign policy on the belief that Middle Eastern terrorists constituted a uniquely dangerous opponent, and he launched what he said would be a long war against them. In some respects, it appeared that the world was back in the realm of history. But the Bush administration's belief that democracy could be implanted quickly in the Arab Middle East, starting with Iraq, testified to a deep conviction that the overall tide of events was running in America's favor.

President Barack Obama built his foreign policy on the conviction that the "war on terror" was overblown, that history really was over, and that, as in the Clinton years, the United States' most important priorities involved promoting the liberal world order, not playing classical geopolitics. The administration articulated an extremely ambitious agenda in support of that order: blocking Iran's drive for nuclear weapons, solving the Israeli-Palestinian conflict, negotiating a global climate change treaty, striking Pacific and Atlantic trade deals, signing arms control treaties with Russia, repairing U.S. relations with the Muslim world, promoting gay rights, restoring trust with European allies, and ending the war in Afghanistan. At the same time, however, Obama planned to cut defense spending dramatically and reduced U.S. engagement in key world theaters, such as Europe and the Middle East.

AN AXIS OF WEEVILS?

All these happy convictions are about to be tested. Twenty-five years after the fall of the Berlin Wall, whether one focuses on the rivalry between the EU and Russia over Ukraine, which led Moscow to seize Crimea; the intensifying competition between China and Japan in East Asia; or the subsuming of sectarian conflict into international rivalries and civil wars in the Middle East, the world is looking less post-historical by the day. In very different ways, with very different objectives, China, Iran, and Russia are all pushing back against the political settlement of the Cold War.

The relationships among those three revisionist powers are complex. In the long run, Russia fears the rise of China. Tehran's worldview has little in common with that of either Beijing or Moscow. Iran and Russia are oil-exporting countries and like the price of oil to be high; China is a net consumer and wants prices low. Political instability in the Middle East can work to Iran's and Russia's advantage but poses large risks for China. One should not speak of a strategic alliance among them, and over time, particularly if they succeed in undermining U.S. influence in Eurasia, the tensions among them are more likely to grow than shrink.

What binds these powers together, however, is their agreement that the status quo must be revised. Russia wants to reassemble as much of the Soviet Union as it can. China has no intention of contenting itself with a secondary role in global affairs, nor will it accept the current degree of U.S. influence in Asia and the territorial status quo there. Iran wishes to replace the current order in the Middle East—led by Saudi Arabia and dominated by Sunni Arab states—with one centered on Tehran.

Leaders in all three countries also agree that U.S. power is the chief obstacle to achieving their revisionist goals. Their hostility toward Washington and its order is both offensive and defensive: not only do they hope that the decline of U.S. power will make it easier to reorder their regions, but they also worry that Washington might try to overthrow them should discord within their countries grow. Yet the revisionists want to avoid direct confrontations with the United States, except in rare circumstances when the odds are strongly in their favor (as in Russia's 2008 invasion of Georgia and its occupation and annexation of Crimea this year). Rather than challenge the status quo head on, they seek to chip away at the norms and relationships that sustain it.

Since Obama has been president, each of these powers has pursued a distinct strategy in light of its own strengths and weaknesses. China, which has the greatest capabilities of the three, has paradoxically been the most frustrated. Its efforts to assert itself in its region have only tightened the links between the United States and its Asian allies and intensified nationalism in Japan. As Beijing's capabilities grow, so will its sense of frustration. China's surge in power will be matched by a surge in Japan's resolve, and tensions in Asia will be more likely to spill over into global economics and politics.

Iran, by many measures the weakest of the three states, has had the most successful record. The combination of the United States' invasion of Iraq and then its premature withdrawal has enabled Tehran to cement deep and enduring ties with significant power centers across the Iraqi border, a development that has changed both the sectarian and the political balance of power in the region. In Syria, Iran, with the help of its longtime ally Hezbollah, has been able to reverse the military tide and prop up the government of Bashar al-Assad in the face of strong opposition from the U.S. government. This triumph of realpolitik has added considerably to Iran's power and prestige. Across the region, the Arab Spring has weakened Sunni regimes, further tilting the balance in Iran's favor. So has the growing split among Sunni governments over what to do about the Muslim Brotherhood and its offshoots and adherents.

Russia, meanwhile, has emerged as the middling revisionist: more powerful than Iran but weaker than China, more successful than China at geopolitics but less successful than Iran. Russia has been moderately effective at driving wedges between Germany and the United States, but Russian President Vladimir Putin's preoccupation with rebuilding the Soviet Union has been hobbled by the sharp limits of his country's economic power. To build a real Eurasian bloc, as Putin dreams of doing, Russia would have to underwrite the bills of the former Soviet republics—something it cannot afford to do.

Nevertheless, Putin, despite his weak hand, has been remarkably successful at frustrating Western projects on former Soviet territory. He has stopped NATO expansion dead in its tracks. He has dismembered Georgia, brought Armenia into his orbit, tightened his hold on Crimea, and, with his Ukrainian adventure, dealt the West an unpleasant and humiliating surprise. From the Western point of view, Putin appears to be condemning his country to an ever-darker future of poverty and marginalization. But Putin doesn't believe that history has ended, and from his perspective, he has solidified his power at home and reminded hostile foreign powers that the Russian bear still has sharp claws.

THE POWERS THAT BE

The revisionist powers have such varied agendas and capabilities that none can provide the kind of systematic and global opposition that the Soviet Union did. As a result, Americans have been slow to realize that these states have undermined the Eurasian geopolitical order in ways that complicate U.S. and European efforts to construct a post-historical, win-win world.

Still, one can see the effects of this revisionist activity in many places. In East Asia, China's increasingly assertive stance has yet to yield much concrete geopolitical progress, but it has fundamentally altered the political dynamic in the region with the fastest-growing economies on earth. Asian politics today revolve around national rivalries, conflicting territorial claims, naval buildups, and similar historical issues. The nationalist revival in Japan, a direct response to China's agenda, has set up a process in which rising nationalism in one country feeds off the same in the other. China and Japan are escalating their rhetoric, increasing their military budgets, starting bilateral crises with greater frequency, and fixating more and more on zero-sum competition.

Although the EU remains in a post-historical moment, the non-EU republics of the former Soviet Union are living in a very different age. In the last few years, hopes of transforming the former Soviet Union into a post-historical region have faded. The Russian occupation of Ukraine is only the latest in a series of steps that have turned eastern Europe into a zone of sharp geopolitical conflict and made stable and effective democratic governance impossible outside the Baltic states and Poland.

In the Middle East, the situation is even more acute. Dreams that the Arab world was approaching a democratic tipping point—dreams that informed U.S. policy under both the Bush and the Obama administrations—have faded. Rather than building a liberal order in the region, U.S. policymakers are grappling with the unraveling of the state system that dates back to the 1916 Sykes-Picot agreement, which divided up the Middle Eastern provinces of the Ottoman Empire, as governance erodes in Iraq, Lebanon, and Syria. Obama has done his best to separate the geopolitical issue of Iran's surging power across the region from the question of its compliance with the Nuclear Nonproliferation Treaty, but Israeli and Saudi fears about Iran's regional ambitions are making that harder to do. Another obstacle to striking agreements with Iran is Russia, which has used its seat on the UN Security Council and support for Assad to set back U.S. goals in Syria.

Russia sees its influence in the Middle East as an important asset in its competition with the United States. This does not mean that Moscow will reflexively oppose U.S. goals on every occasion, but it does mean that the win-win outcomes that Americans so eagerly seek will sometimes be held hostage to Russian geopolitical interests. In deciding how hard to press Russia over Ukraine, for example, the White House cannot avoid calculating the impact on Russia's stance on the Syrian war or Iran's nuclear program. Russia cannot make itself a richer country or a much larger one, but it has made itself a more important factor in U.S. strategic thinking, and it can use that leverage to extract concessions that matter to it.

If these revisionist powers have gained ground, the status quo powers have been undermined. The deterioration is sharpest in Europe, where the unmitigated disaster of the common currency has divided public opinion and turned the EU's attention in on itself. The EU may have avoided the worst possible consequences of the euro crisis, but both its will and its capacity for effective action beyond its frontiers have been significantly impaired.

The United States has not suffered anything like the economic pain much of Europe has gone through, but with the country facing the foreign policy hangover induced by the Bush-era wars, an increasingly intrusive surveillance state, a slow economic recovery, and an unpopular health-care law, the public mood has soured. On both the left and the right, Americans are questioning the benefits of the current world order and the competence of its architects. Additionally, the public shares the elite consensus that in a post–Cold War world, the United States ought to be able to pay less into the system and get more out. When that doesn't happen, people blame their leaders. In any case, there is little public appetite for large new initiatives at home or abroad, and a cynical public is turning away from a polarized Washington with a mix of boredom and disdain.

Obama came into office planning to cut military spending and reduce the importance of foreign policy in American politics while strengthening the liberal world order. A little more than halfway through his presidency, he finds himself increasingly bogged down in exactly the kinds of geopolitical rivalries he had hoped to transcend. Chinese, Iranian, and Russian revanchism haven't overturned the post–Cold War settlement in Eurasia yet, and may never do so, but they have converted an uncontested status quo into a contested one. U.S. presidents no longer have a free hand as they seek to deepen the liberal system; they are increasingly concerned with shoring up its geopolitical foundations.

THE TWILIGHT OF HISTORY

It was 22 years ago that Fukuyama published The End of History and the Last Man, and it is tempting to see the return of geopolitics as a definitive refutation of his thesis. The reality is more complicated. The end of history, as Fukuyama reminded readers, was

Hegel's idea, and even though the revolutionary state had triumphed over the old type of regimes for good, Hegel argued, competition and conflict would continue. He predicted that there would be disturbances in the provinces, even as the heartlands of European civilization moved into a post-historical time. Given that Hegel's provinces included China, India, Japan, and Russia, it should hardly be surprising that more than two centuries later, the disturbances haven't ceased. We are living in the twilight of history rather than at its actual end.

A Hegelian view of the historical process today would hold that substantively little has changed since the beginning of the nineteenth century. To be powerful, states must develop the ideas and institutions that allow them to harness the titanic forces of industrial and informational capitalism. There is no alternative; societies unable or unwilling to embrace this route will end up the subjects of history rather than the makers of it.

But the road to postmodernity remains rocky. In order to increase its power, China, for example, will clearly have to go through a process of economic and political development that will require the country to master the problems that modern Western societies have confronted. There is no assurance, however, that China's path to stable liberal modernity will be any less tumultuous than, say, the one that Germany trod. The twilight of history is not a quiet time.

The second part of Fukuyama's book has received less attention, perhaps because it is less flattering to the West. As Fukuyama investigated what a post-historical society would look like, he made a disturbing discovery. In a world where the great questions have been solved and geopolitics has been subordinated to economics, humanity will look a lot like the nihilistic "last man" described by the philosopher Friedrich Nietzsche: a narcissistic consumer with no greater aspirations beyond the next trip to the mall.

In other words, these people would closely resemble today's European bureaucrats and Washington lobbyists. They are competent enough at managing their affairs among post-historical people, but understanding the motives and countering the strategies of old-fashioned power politicians is hard for them. Unlike their less productive and less stable rivals, post-historical people are unwilling to make sacrifices, focused on the short term, easily distracted, and lacking in courage.

The realities of personal and political life in post-historical societies are very different from those in such countries as China, Iran, and Russia, where the sun of history still shines. It is not just that those different societies bring different personalities and values to the fore; it is also that their institutions work differently and their publics are shaped by different ideas.

Societies filled with Nietzsche's last men (and women) characteristically misunderstand and underestimate their supposedly primitive opponents in supposedly backward societies—a blind spot that could, at least temporarily, offset their countries' other advantages. The tide of history may be flowing inexorably in the direction of liberal capitalist democracy, and the sun of history may indeed be sinking behind the hills. But even as the shadows lengthen and the first of the stars appears, such figures as Putin still stride the world stage. They will not go gentle into that good night, and they will rage, rage against the dying of the light.

WALTER RUSSELL MEAD is James Clarke Chace Professor of Foreign Affairs and Humanities at Bard College and Editor-at-Large of The American Interest. Follow him on Twitter @wrmead.

The Illusion of Geopolitics

The Enduring Power of the Liberal Order

G. John Ikenberry   FROM OUR MAY/JUNE 2014 ISSUE

Transnational anthem: pro-EU demonstrators singing in Kiev, November 2013. (Stoyan Nenov / Courtesy Reuters)

Walter Russell Mead paints a disturbing portrait of the United States' geopolitical predicament. As he sees it, an increasingly formidable coalition of illiberal powers—China, Iran, and Russia—is determined to undo the post–Cold War settlement and the U.S.-led global order that stands behind it. Across Eurasia, he argues, these aggrieved states are bent on building spheres of influence to threaten the foundations of U.S. leadership and the global order. So the United States must rethink its optimism, including its post–Cold War belief that rising non-Western states can be persuaded to join the West and play by its rules. For Mead, the time has come to confront the threats from these increasingly dangerous geopolitical foes.

But Mead's alarmism is based on a colossal misreading of modern power realities. It is a misreading of the logic and character of the existing world order, which is more stable and expansive than Mead depicts, leading him to overestimate the ability of the "axis of weevils" to undermine it. And it is a misreading of China and Russia, which are not full-scale revisionist powers but part-time spoilers at best, as suspicious of each other as they are of the outside world. True, they look for opportunities to resist the United States' global leadership, and recently, as in the past, they have pushed back against it, particularly when confronted in their own neighborhoods. But even these conflicts are fueled more by weakness—their leaders' and regimes'—than by strength. They have no appealing brand. And when it comes to their overriding interests, Russia and, especially, China are deeply integrated into the world economy and its governing institutions.

Mead also mischaracterizes the thrust of U.S. foreign policy. Since the end of the Cold War, he argues, the United States has ignored geopolitical issues involving territory and spheres of influence and instead adopted a Pollyannaish emphasis on building the global order. But this is a false dichotomy. The United States does not focus on issues of global order, such as arms control and trade, because it assumes that geopolitical conflict is gone forever; it undertakes such efforts precisely because it wants to manage great-power competition. Order building is not premised on the end of geopolitics; it is about how to answer the big questions of geopolitics.

Indeed, the construction of a U.S.-led global order did not begin with the end of the Cold War; it won the Cold War. In the nearly 70 years since World War II, Washington has undertaken sustained efforts to build a far-flung system of multilateral institutions, alliances, trade agreements, and political partnerships. This project has helped draw countries into the United States' orbit. It has helped strengthen global norms and rules that undercut the legitimacy of nineteenth-century-style spheres of influence, bids for regional domination, and territorial grabs. And it has given the United States the capacities, partnerships, and principles to confront today's great-power spoilers and revisionists, such as they are. Alliances, partnerships, multilateralism, democracy—these are the tools of U.S. leadership, and they are winning, not losing, the twenty-first-century struggles over geopolitics and the world order.

THE GENTLE GIANT

In 1904, the English geographer Halford Mackinder wrote that the great power that controlled the heartland of Eurasia would command "the World-Island" and thus the world itself. For Mead, Eurasia has returned as the great prize of geopolitics. Across the far reaches of this supercontinent, he argues, China, Iran, and Russia are seeking to establish their spheres of influence and challenge U.S. interests, slowly but relentlessly attempting to dominate Eurasia and thereby threaten the United States and the rest of the world.

This vision misses a deeper reality. In matters of geopolitics (not to mention demographics, politics, and ideas), the United States has a decisive advantage over China, Iran, and Russia. Although the United States will no doubt come down from the peak of hegemony that it occupied during the unipolar era, its power is still unrivaled. Its wealth and technological advantages remain far out of the reach of China and Russia, to say nothing of Iran. Its recovering economy, now bolstered by massive new natural gas resources, allows it to maintain a global military presence and credible security commitments.

Indeed, Washington enjoys a unique ability to win friends and influence states. According to a study led by the political scientist Brett Ashley Leeds, the United States boasts military partnerships with more than 60 countries, whereas Russia counts eight formal allies and China has just one (North Korea). As one British diplomat told me several years ago, "China doesn't seem to do alliances."

But the United States does, and they pay a double dividend: not only do alliances provide a global platform for the projection of U.S. power, but they also distribute the burden of providing security. The military capabilities aggregated in this U.S.-led alliance system outweigh anything China or Russia might generate for decades to come.

Then there are the nuclear weapons. These arms, which the United States, China, and Russia all possess (and Iran is seeking), help the United States in two ways. First, thanks to the logic of mutual assured destruction, they radically reduce the likelihood of great-power war. Such upheavals have provided opportunities for past great powers, including the United States in World War II, to entrench their own international orders. The atomic age has robbed China and Russia of this opportunity. Second, nuclear weapons also make China and Russia more secure, giving them assurance that the United States will never invade. That's a good thing, because it reduces the likelihood that they will resort to desperate moves, born of insecurity, that risk war and undermine the liberal order.

Geography reinforces the United States' other advantages. As the only great power not surrounded by other great powers, the country has appeared less threatening to other states and was able to rise dramatically over the course of the last century without triggering a war. After the Cold War, when the United States was the world's sole superpower, other global powers, oceans away, did not even attempt to balance against it. In fact, the United States' geographic position has led other countries to worry more about abandonment than domination. Allies in Europe, Asia, and the Middle East have sought to draw the United States into playing a greater role in their regions. The result is what the historian Geir Lundestad has called an "empire by invitation."

The United States' geographic advantage is on full display in Asia. Most countries there see China as a greater potential danger—due to its proximity, if nothing else—than the United States. Except for the United States, every major power in the world lives in a crowded geopolitical neighborhood where shifts in power routinely provoke counterbalancing—including by one another. China is discovering this dynamic today as surrounding states react to its rise by modernizing their militaries and reinforcing their alliances. Russia has known it for decades, and has faced it most recently in Ukraine, which in recent years has increased its military spending and sought closer ties to the EU.

Geographic isolation has also given the United States reason to champion universal principles that allow it to access various regions of the world. The country has long promoted the open-door policy and the principle of self-determination and opposed colonialism—less out of a sense of idealism than due to the practical realities of keeping Europe, Asia, and the Middle East open for trade and diplomacy. In the late 1930s, the main question facing the United States was how large a geopolitical space, or "grand area," it would need to exist as a great power in a world of empires, regional blocs, and spheres of influence. World War II made the answer clear: the country's prosperity and security depended on access to every region. And in the ensuing decades, with some important and damaging exceptions, such as Vietnam, the United States has embraced postimperial principles.

It was during these postwar years that geopolitics and order building converged. A liberal international framework was the answer that statesmen such as Dean Acheson, George Kennan, and George Marshall offered to the challenge of Soviet expansionism. The system they built strengthened and enriched the United States and its allies, to the detriment of its illiberal opponents. It also stabilized the world economy and established mechanisms for tackling global problems. The end of the Cold War has not changed the logic behind this project.

Fortunately, the liberal principles that Washington has pushed enjoy near-universal appeal, because they have tended to be a good fit with the modernizing forces of economic growth and social advancement. As the historian Charles Maier has put it, the United States surfed the wave of twentieth-century modernization. But some have argued that this congruence between the American project and the forces of modernity has weakened in recent years. The 2008 financial crisis, the thinking goes, marked a world-historical turning point, at which the United States lost its vanguard role in facilitating economic advancement.

Yet even if that were true, it hardly follows that China and Russia have replaced the United States as the standard-bearers of the global economy. Even Mead does not argue that China, Iran, or Russia offers the world a new model of modernity. If these illiberal powers really do threaten Washington and the rest of the liberal capitalist world, then they will need to find and ride the next great wave of modernization. They are unlikely to do that.

THE RISE OF DEMOCRACY

Mead's vision of a contest over Eurasia between the United States and China, Iran, and Russia misses the more profound power transition under way: the increasing ascendancy of liberal capitalist democracy. To be sure, many liberal democracies are struggling at the moment with slow economic growth, social inequality, and political instability. But the spread of liberal democracy throughout the world, beginning in the late 1970s and accelerating after the Cold War, has dramatically strengthened the United States' position and tightened the geopolitical circle around China and Russia.

It's easy to forget how rare liberal democracy once was. Until the twentieth century, it was confined to the West and parts of Latin America. After World War II, however, it began to reach beyond those realms, as newly independent states established self-rule. During the 1950s, 1960s, and early 1970s, military coups and new dictators put the brakes on democratic transitions. But in the late 1970s, what the political scientist Samuel Huntington termed "the third wave" of democratization washed over southern Europe, Latin America, and East Asia. Then the Cold War ended, and a cohort of former communist states in eastern Europe were brought into the democratic fold. By the late 1990s, 60 percent of all countries had become democracies.

Although some backsliding has occurred, the more significant trend has been the emergence of a group of democratic middle powers, including Australia, Brazil, India, Indonesia, Mexico, South Korea, and Turkey. These rising democracies are acting as stakeholders in the international system: pushing for multilateral cooperation, seeking greater rights and responsibilities, and exercising influence through peaceful means.

Such countries lend the liberal world order new geopolitical heft. As the political scientist Larry Diamond has noted, if Argentina, Brazil, India, Indonesia, South Africa, and Turkey regain their economic footing and strengthen their democratic rule, the G-20, which also includes the United States and European countries, "will have become a strong 'club of democracies,' with only Russia, China, and Saudi Arabia holding out." The rise of a global middle class of democratic states has turned China and Russia into outliers—not, as Mead fears, legitimate contestants for global leadership.

In fact, the democratic upsurge has been deeply problematic for both countries. In eastern Europe, former Soviet states and satellites have gone democratic and joined the West. As worrisome as Russian President Vladimir Putin's moves in Crimea have been, they reflect Russia's geopolitical vulnerability, not its strength. Over the last two decades, the West has crept closer to Russia's borders. In 1999, the Czech Republic, Hungary, and Poland entered NATO. They were joined in 2004 by seven more former members of the Soviet bloc, and in 2009, by Albania and Croatia. In the meantime, six former Soviet republics have headed down the path to membership by joining NATO's Partnership for Peace program. Mead makes much of Putin's achievements in Georgia, Armenia, and Crimea. Yet even though Putin is winning some small battles, he is losing the war. Russia is not on the rise; to the contrary, it is experiencing one of the greatest geopolitical contractions of any major power in the modern era.

Democracy is encircling China, too. In the mid-1980s, India and Japan were the only Asian democracies, but since then, Indonesia, Mongolia, the Philippines, South Korea, Taiwan, and Thailand have joined the club. Myanmar (also called Burma) has made cautious steps toward multiparty rule—steps that have come, as China has not failed to notice, in conjunction with warming relations with the United States. China now lives in a decidedly democratic neighborhood.

These political transformations have put China and Russia on the defensive. Consider the recent developments in Ukraine. The economic and political currents in most of the country are inexorably flowing westward, a trend that terrifies Putin. His only recourse has been to strong-arm Ukraine into resisting the EU and remaining in Russia's orbit. Although he may be able to keep Crimea under Russian control, his grip on the rest of the country is slipping. As the EU diplomat Robert Cooper has noted, Putin can try to delay the moment when Ukraine "affiliates with the EU, but he can't stop it." Indeed, Putin might not even be able to accomplish that, since his provocative moves may serve only to speed Ukraine's move toward Europe.

China faces a similar predicament in Taiwan. Chinese leaders sincerely believe that Taiwan is part of China, but the Taiwanese do not. The democratic transition on the island has made its inhabitants' claims to nationhood more deeply felt and legitimate. A 2011 survey found that if the Taiwanese could be assured that China would not attack Taiwan, 80 percent of them would support declaring independence. Like Russia, China wants geopolitical control over its neighborhood. But the spread of democracy to all corners of Asia has made old-fashioned domination the only way to achieve that, and that option is costly and self-defeating.

While the rise of democratic states makes life more difficult for China and Russia, it makes the world safer for the United States. Those two powers may count as U.S. rivals, but the rivalry takes place on a very uneven playing field: the United States has the most friends, and the most capable ones, too. Washington and its allies account for 75 percent of global military spending. Democratization has put China and Russia in a geopolitical box.

Iran is not surrounded by democracies, but it is threatened by a restive pro-democracy movement at home. More important, Iran is the weakest member of Mead's axis, with a much smaller economy and military than the United States and the other great powers. It is also the target of the strongest international sanctions regime ever assembled, with help from China and Russia. The Obama administration's diplomacy with Iran may or may not succeed, but it is not clear what Mead would do differently to prevent the country from acquiring nuclear weapons. U.S. President Barack Obama's approach has the virtue of offering Tehran a path by which it can move from being a hostile regional power to becoming a more constructive, nonnuclear member of the international community—a potential geopolitical game changer that Mead fails to appreciate.

REVISIONISM REVISITED

Not only does Mead underestimate the strength of the United States and the order it built; he also overstates the degree to which China and Russia are seeking to resist both. (Apart from its nuclear ambitions, Iran looks like a state engaged more in futile protest than actual resistance, so it shouldn't be considered anything close to a revisionist power.) Without a doubt, China and Russia desire greater regional influence. China has made aggressive claims over maritime rights and nearby contested islands, and it has embarked on an arms buildup. Putin has visions of reclaiming Russia's dominance in its "near abroad." Both great powers bristle at U.S. leadership and resist it when they can.

But China and Russia are not true revisionists. As former Israeli Foreign Minister Shlomo Ben-Ami has said, Putin's foreign policy is "more a reflection of his resentment of Russia's geopolitical marginalization than a battle cry from a rising empire." China, of course, is an actual rising power, and this does invite dangerous competition with U.S. allies in Asia. But China is not currently trying to break those alliances or overthrow the wider system of regional security governance embodied in the Association of Southeast Asian Nations and the East Asia Summit. And even if China harbors ambitions of eventually doing so, U.S. security partnerships in the region are, if anything, getting stronger, not weaker. At most, China and Russia are spoilers. They do not have the interests—let alone the ideas, capacities, or allies—to lead them to upend existing global rules and institutions.

In fact, although they resent that the United States stands at the top of the current geopolitical system, they embrace the underlying logic of that framework, and with good reason. Openness gives them access to trade, investment, and technology from other societies. Rules give them tools to protect their sovereignty and interests. Despite controversies over the new idea of "the responsibility to protect" (which has been applied only selectively), the current world order enshrines the age-old norms of state sovereignty and nonintervention. Those Westphalian principles remain the bedrock of world politics—and China and Russia have tied their national interests to them (despite Putin's disturbing irredentism).

It should come as no surprise, then, that China and Russia have become deeply integrated into the existing international order. They are both permanent members of the UN Security Council, with veto rights, and they both participate actively in the World Trade Organization, the International Monetary Fund, the World Bank, and the G-20. They are geopolitical insiders, sitting at all the high tables of global governance.

China, despite its rapid ascent, has no ambitious global agenda; it remains fixated inward, on preserving party rule. Some Chinese intellectuals and political figures, such as Yan Xuetong and Zhu Chenghu, do have a wish list of revisionist goals. They see the Western system as a threat and are waiting for the day when China can reorganize the international order. But these voices do not reach very far into the political elite. Indeed, Chinese leaders have moved away from their earlier calls for sweeping change. In 2007, at its Central Committee meeting, the Chinese Communist Party replaced previous proposals for a "new international economic order" with calls for more modest reforms centering on fairness and justice. The Chinese scholar Wang Jisi has argued that this move is "subtle but important," shifting China's orientation toward that of a global reformer. China now wants a larger role in the International Monetary Fund and the World Bank, greater voice in such forums as the G-20, and wider global use of its currency. That is not the agenda of a country trying to revise the economic order.

China and Russia are also members in good standing of the nuclear club. The centerpiece of the Cold War settlement between the United States and the Soviet Union (and then Russia) was a shared effort to limit atomic weapons. Although U.S.-Russian relations have since soured, the nuclear component of their arrangement has held. In 2010, Moscow and Washington signed the New START treaty, which requires mutual reductions in long-range nuclear weapons.

Before the 1990s, China was a nuclear outsider. Although it had a modest arsenal, it saw itself as a voice of the nonnuclear developing world and criticized arms control agreements and test bans. But in a remarkable shift, China has since come to support the array of nuclear accords, including the Nuclear Nonproliferation Treaty and the Comprehensive Nuclear Test Ban Treaty. It has affirmed a "no first use" doctrine, kept its arsenal small, and taken its entire nuclear force off alert. China has also played an active role in the Nuclear Security Summit, an initiative proposed by Obama in 2009, and it has joined the "P5 process," a collaborate effort to safeguard nuclear weapons.

Across a wide range of issues, China and Russia are acting more like established great powers than revisionist ones. They often choose to shun multilateralism, but so, too, on occasion do the United States and other powerful democracies. (Beijing has ratified the UN Convention on the Law of the Sea; Washington has not.) And China and Russia are using global rules and institutions to advance their own interests. Their struggles with the United States revolve around gaining voice within the existing order and manipulating it to suit their needs. They wish to enhance their positions within the system, but they are not trying to replace it.

HERE TO STAY

Ultimately, even if China and Russia do attempt to contest the basic terms of the current global order, the adventure will be daunting and self-defeating. These powers aren't just up against the United States; they would also have to contend with the most globally organized and deeply entrenched order the world has ever seen, one that is dominated by states that are liberal, capitalist, and democratic. This order is backed by a U.S.-led network of alliances, institutions, geopolitical bargains, client states, and democratic partnerships. It has proved dynamic and expansive, easily integrating rising states, beginning with Japan and Germany after World War II. It has shown a capacity for shared leadership, as exemplified by such forums as the G-8 and the G-20. It has allowed rising non-Western countries to trade and grow, sharing the dividends of modernization. It has accommodated a surprisingly wide variety of political and economic models—social democratic (western Europe), neoliberal (the United Kingdom and the United States), and state capitalist (East Asia). The prosperity of nearly every country—and the stability of its government—fundamentally depends on this order.

In the age of liberal order, revisionist struggles are a fool's errand. Indeed, China and Russia know this. They do not have grand visions of an alternative order. For them, international relations are mainly about the search for commerce and resources, the protection of their sovereignty, and, where possible, regional domination. They have shown no interest in building their own orders or even taking full responsibility for the current one and have offered no alternative visions of global economic or political progress. That's a critical shortcoming, since international orders rise and fall not simply with the power of the leading state; their success also hinges on whether they are seen as legitimate and whether their actual operation solves problems that both weak and powerful states care about. In the struggle for world order, China and Russia (and certainly Iran) are simply not in the game.

Under these circumstances, the United States should not give up its efforts to strengthen the liberal order. The world that Washington inhabits today is one it should welcome. And the grand strategy it should pursue is the one it has followed for decades: deep global engagement. It is a strategy in which the United States ties itself to the regions of the world through trade, alliances, multilateral institutions, and diplomacy. It is a strategy in which the United States establishes leadership not simply through the exercise of power but also through sustained efforts at global problem solving and rule making. It created a world that is friendly to American interests, and it is made friendly because, as President John F. Kennedy once said, it is a world "where the weak are safe and the strong are just."

G. JOHN IKENBERRY is Albert G. Milbank Professor of Politics and International Affairs at Princeton University and George Eastman Visiting Professor at Balliol College, University of Oxford.

Show Them the Money

Why Giving Cash Helps Alleviate Poverty

Christopher Blattman
and Paul Niehaus   FROM OUR MAY/JUNE 2014 ISSUE

Girls walk in a slum on the outskirts of Islamabad, February 4, 2014. (Zohra Bensemra / Courtesy Reuters)

Every year, wealthy countries spend billions of dollars to help the world's poor, paying for cows, goats, seeds, beans, textbooks, business training, microloans, and much more. Such aid is designed to give poor people things they can't afford or the tools and skills to earn more. Much of this aid undoubtedly works. But even when assistance programs accomplish things, they often do so in a tremendously expensive and inefficient way. Part of this is due to overhead, but overhead costs get far more attention than they deserve. More worrisome is the actual price of procuring and giving away goats, textbooks, sacks of beans, and the like.

Most development agencies either fail to track their costs precisely or keep their accounting books confidential, but a number of candid organizations have opened themselves up to scrutiny. Their experiences suggest that delivering stuff to the poor is a lot more expensive than one might expect.

Take cows. Many Western organizations give poor families livestock, along with training in how to raise and profit from the animals. Cows themselves usually cost no more than a few hundred dollars each, but delivering them—targeting recipients, administering the donations, transporting the animals—gets expensive. In West Bengal, India, for example, the nonprofit Bandhan spends $331 to get $166 worth of local livestock and other assets to the poor, according to a report by the rating agency Micro-Credit Ratings International. Yet even this program sounds like a bargain compared to others. In Rwanda, a study led by the economist Rosemary Rawlins found that the cost of donating a pregnant cow, with attendant training classes and support services, through the charity Heifer International can reach $3,000.

Such programs surely reduce poverty: having a cow is undoubtedly better than not having one. But they also carry an opportunity cost, since the money spent on procuring and delivering the cows or other assets could instead go directly to the poor. Bandhan, for example, could give twice as many households cash grants equal to the local price of the livestock it now gives as it does actual livestock. And in place of each cow it provides, Heifer could give $300—roughly half of Rwanda's per capita income—to ten poor families.

Does the benefit of an in-kind donation to one family really outweigh the value of helping twice or even ten times as many households? For a growing number of antipoverty programs, the answer to that question appears to be no. New research suggests that cash grants to the poor are as good as or better than many traditional forms of aid when it comes to reducing poverty. The process of transferring cash, moreover, is only getting cheaper, thanks to the spread of technologies such as cell phones and satellite signals. And simply asking whether a given program is doing more good than it costs puts pressure on the aid sector to be more transparent and accountable. It's well past time, then, for donors to stop thinking of unconditional cash payments as an oddball policy and start seeing them for what they are: one of the most sensible tools of poverty alleviation.

MONEY MATTERS

When it comes to deciding how to help the poor, the stakes couldn't be higher. Each year, U.S. households donate at least $15 billion abroad. Their government gives $30 billion in foreign aid, and wealthy states collectively give $150 billion in development aid. Yet the world's poorest people receive very little of that money in actual cash.

"Just give the poor cash" is an old refrain. What is new, however, is a burgeoning body of experimental evidence, produced by groups ranging from the nonprofit Innovations for Poverty Action to the World Bank, on how the effect of cash grants compares to that of in-kind donations. Recent studies have come to surprising conclusions, finding that typically lauded approaches to reducing poverty, such as educational and loan programs, are not so effective after all.

One of the best examples is microloans, small, short-term loans to poor entrepreneurs. By opening up credit to people who were too poor to borrow from banks, the logic went, microfinance would give the poor the jump-start they needed to escape their plight. Beginning in the 1990s, the microcredit movement took the development world by storm, leading to a Nobel Peace Prize for the Bangladesh-based Grameen Bank in 2006.

Yet a belated series of randomized trials has called the success of microloans into question. One example comes from the Indian nonprofit Spandana. Beginning in 2005, the group made loans of about $250 to hundreds of women in Hyderabad, India, at relatively low interest rates. The MIT economist Abhijit Banerjee and a number of collaborators worked with Spandana to evaluate the program's performance over three years; they found no effect on education, health, poverty, or women's empowerment. To be sure, people certainly benefit from access to credit; it helps them cope with crises and buy expensive things such as new roofs or farm equipment and pay for them over time. But as Banerjee concluded after reviewing an additional two decades' worth of data on such loans, "there is no evidence of large sustained consumption or income gains as a result of access to microcredit."

Another popular approach to development aid has been business and vocational training. There is little data on how much aid spending goes to training, but as an example, the International Labor Organization's Start and Improve Your Business Program claims to have trained more than 4.5 million people in over 100 countries since 1977. "Teach a man to fish and you feed him for a lifetime," the proverb goes. Yet the results of teaching anything—be it fishing or farming or word processing—have been patchy at best. In 2012, the economists David McKenzie and Christopher Woodruff reviewed more than a dozen randomized trials in developing countries and concluded that training business owners had little lasting effect on their sales or profits.

No wonder people in developing countries, when given the choice, don't necessarily choose to invest in skills training. In another recent study, one of us (Christopher Blattman) worked with the economists Nathan Fiala and Sebastian Martinez to examine a government-run training program in Uganda. Rather than simply providing classes in various trades, the initiative gave grants of around $7,000 to over 250 groups of 15–25 young adults (roughly $400 per group member) in return for a simple business plan describing how they would use the money to buy vocational training and tools. The groups were otherwise free to spend the money without oversight. The majority of the participants ended up using the funding to enter skilled trades such as tailoring or metalworking. But they spent most of the money acquiring the physical tools and materials they needed to start working, allocating only around ten percent of the grants to training. That turned out to be a wise investment decision: over four years, the participants' incomes rose by an average of roughly 40 percent.

None of this is to say that existing practices should be tossed aside. But they can certainly be improved. With microfinance, for example, finding ways of lending larger sums for longer periods at lower rates would surely make many businesses more sustainable and profitable. The key point, however, is that new data are challenging the conventional wisdom that has long dictated how billions in development dollars are spent. Simply having a plausible theory of change doesn't cut it anymore. These days, it's about providing evidence of change—especially change that justifies the price of bringing it about.

DON'T HAVE A COW, MAN

Over the past few years, it has become increasingly clear that giving away money works in a wide range of development situations. Mexican families, Ghanaian farmers, Kenyan villagers, Malawian schoolgirls, and war-affected Ugandans—all have been shown in randomized trials to benefit from cash transfers. Economists have studied money transfers with conditions and without conditions, under supervision and not under supervision, on large scales and small scales, and against comparable loans. And by testing the effects of handouts over unusually long periods of time—five years out in Sri Lanka, four years out in Uganda—scholars have had access to far more detailed data than is available for many other poverty-reduction strategies.

These findings are particularly important because many funders, including governments, aid organizations, and development professionals, still harbor significant reservations about cash transfers. They raise a variety of familiar concerns: that men drink their cash away, that the diligent but uneducated poor struggle to make sound decisions, and that handouts make people ever more dependent on aid. So far, however, the data contradict the most pessimistic of these worries.

Studies have shown that the world's poorest people do not squander cash transfers, even when there are no strings attached. An extreme example comes from a recent experiment run by one of us (Blattman), Julian Jamison, and Margaret Sheridan. In 2010–13, we gave unconditional grants of $200 to some of the least disciplined men to be found: drug addicts and petty criminals in the slums of Liberia. Bucking expectations, these recipients did not waste the money, instead spending the majority of the funds on basic necessities or starting their own businesses. If these men didn't throw away free money, who would?

That finding echoes similar results elsewhere. Study after study has shown that recipients of cash grants invest the money or spend it on such basic items as food and better shelter. Poor people don't always make the best choices with their money, of course, but fears that they consistently waste it are simply not borne out in the available data.

Nor is there evidence that unconditional cash transfers make recipients lazy. Especially for poor people who have not fulfilled their potential, such as small-business owners or underemployed youth with little access to hard capital, cash grants have frequently created wealth. Using such donations, entrepreneurs in Ghana and Sri Lanka have expanded their businesses, displaced women in Uganda have become traders and doubled their earnings, and farmers in Kenya have made home investments with high returns. In most of these experiments, people increased their future earning potential over the long term. In some cases, they did not. But in every study, people worked at least as many hours in the labor force as they had before receiving the cash transfers, if not more.

In some ways, the new research on cash transfers actually affirms the wisdom of traditional approaches to development assistance. Poor people in developing countries often use the cash given them to buy the same things that aid organizations have traditionally provided—livestock, tools, training, and so on. No one living on less than $2 a day says no to a free cow, even if he is not cut out to be a dairy farmer. But the advantage of cash is its flexibility. When people have cash in hand, they tend to buy a wider variety of goods and services. Not everyone, after all, wants a cow.

THE FUTURE OF GIVING

This abundance of data suggests that people are poor not because they lack initiative but because they lack resources and opportunities—things that, in many places, money can buy. Donors should thus ask themselves: With each dollar we spend, are we doing more good than the poor could do on their own with the same dollar?

In 2010–11, the Association of Volunteers in International Service, a Catholic development organization, did just that, evaluating an ongoing program in postwar northern Uganda in real time. To help 1,800 of the country's poorest women become retailers and traders, the program had been providing each woman with a grant of $150, five days of business planning assistance and training, and follow-up visits from aid workers who offered supervision and advice. Altogether, the program cost nearly $700 for every impoverished woman it assisted. The organization, working with a team of researchers that included one of us (Blattman), decided to measure the impact of the program without its most expensive service: the follow-up visits. We found that such visits did increase the women's profits yet cost more than twice the amount of the cash grant itself. In other words, the follow-up was far less effective per dollar than the grant and the training course.

One potential response would have been to cut the follow-up service and give out larger cash grants. But in this case, the organization plans to find a way to provide the extra services more cheaply. This will prove a high bar to meet, but either way, the end result will be that it gets more bang for its buck.

The Ugandan example illustrates another upside to cash transfers: they can serve as the index funds of international development. An index fund is a bundle of investments that is not actively managed, reducing the costs for investors. Its value simply reflects the upward and downward swings of the individual stocks that are included in the bundle. Similarly, a cash transfer is a development project stripped of any active management costs, and its performance tracks the success or failure of the individual recipient. Cash transfers thus provide a baseline for evaluating the active management performance of government officials and development professionals. Unfortunately, the sort of hard-nosed performance review seen in the Ugandan study—let alone the courage and discipline required for any organization to put its core competencies to the test—remains rare.

Still, the studies so far, plus basic economic reasoning, suggest three predictions about how cash will perform relative to traditional aid programs. First, money transfers will likely prove most valuable in places where the population has been hit hard by unexpected crises—countries or regions recovering from violent conflicts, natural disasters, or extended periods of political uncertainty. Think of Southeast Asia after a tsunami or the Middle East flooded with Syrian refugees, where the returns on capital after a recovery period are likely to be unusually high and the challenge of making smart investments without localized knowledge unusually large.

Second, cash could also excel in places such as Ghana, Kenya, or Uganda—reasonably stable, growing countries that happen to have few firms offering jobs and where most workers, by necessity, are self-employed. Here, many of the poor are working below their potential because they lack the capital, credit, or insurance products necessary to grow their businesses. In the absence of financial services, which can take decades to develop, cash can fill the gap.

Third, the forms of aid most likely to outperform cash will be those that address collective problems, or what economists term "public goods." Consider health, for example. Say you were buying a vaccine to reduce your child's risk of getting sick. A big part of the social value of this purchase would be reducing your neighbors' risk of illness, too. If you had little cash to spare, the vaccine might cost more than it was worth to you but less than it was worth to the community at large. In this case, an outside group would be better placed to tend to the greater good by subsidizing the vaccine or even providing it for free. A cash transfer wouldn't solve the social problem if the recipient had more pressing needs to spend the money on than the vaccine.

In many cases, however, Western officials and organizations are not the best judges of what poor people in developing countries need to make a better living; the poor people themselves are. One of us (Paul Niehaus), working with fellow economists Karthik Muralidharan and Sandip Sukhtankar, is currently conducting an unusual poll in rural Bihar, India. We are giving poor citizens a choice between two types of aid: the assistance provided by the government's Public Distribution System, a venerable program of subsidized food delivery that consumes nearly one percent of India's GDP, or cash transfers, calibrated to cost the government the same amount per family. Both forms of welfare have their advantages. Direct cash transfers bypass corrupt officials and crafty middlemen, whereas food transfers provide a more reliable form of insurance against rising food prices. The results are not yet in, but the experiment should provide a promising model for determining how to spend aid dollars in the future.

Such exercises have their limitations, of course, but they also have the advantage of linking smart policy with smart politics. Offering citizens their choice of programs gives elected officials the kind of insight they crave: raw data that describe what voters want and whether or not the civil service is delivering it. Like cash transfers themselves, such mechanisms can help make aid delivery more accountable to the people the aid is intended to serve.

CASHING IN

Despite everything that cash transfers can do, their future role in poverty alleviation remains uncertain. The findings of small-scale experiments, involving just a few thousand recipients, cannot reliably tell what might happen when the same policies are rolled out to millions. One looming question is whether money transfers are more or less feasible on a large scale than traditional programs—whether,

45

for example, corrupt officials and armed groups could exploit such programs more easily.

But the evidence from countries that already use cash transfers on a massive scale is promising. According to the United Kingdom's Department for International Development, governments in the developing world already run cash-transfer programs that reach between 750 million and one billion people, whether by way of employment programs in India, pension funds in South Africa, or welfare schemes in Brazil. Many of these programs involve some kind of condition that must be met before recipients get paid, such as getting a checkup or a vaccine at a health clinic. But they all end in cash transfers. The worst fears surrounding them—of fraud, corruption, and plain ineffectiveness—have thus far not been realized.

New technologies have also made such programs easier to implement. In India, one of us (Niehaus), along with Muralidharan and Sukhtankar, recently worked with the government of the state of Andhra Pradesh to measure the effects of replacing paper money delivered through the mail to pensioners and workfare participants with digital payments using biometric authentication. We found that the new system both reduced theft and improved the speed and reliability of the payments. Taking this approach further, the nonprofit GiveDirectly (of which Niehaus is president) now delivers unconditional cash payments to thousands of extremely poor households in East Africa through accounts on their cell phones, all at a cost of less than ten cents per dollar donated.

Another concern about rolling out cash transfers on a large scale in developing economies is that an influx of money could lead to disruptive inflation. Whether that fear will materialize remains unclear. It will depend in large part on what the macroeconomic effects of cash transfers are compared to—whether food aid, universal education, or other goods and services. Any large-scale influx of goods or currency has the potential to be disruptive, and so the real question is whether giving cash is worse than giving something else.

Economic theory and experience provide some reassurance. Consider the hundreds of thousands of Syrian refugees now living in Lebanon, where the United Nations and humanitarian agencies are dispensing cash via ATM cards as the main form of relief. In such open economies, cash should have little effect on food prices or supplies, and it could even stimulate local production. But when it comes to goods that are slow to keep up with demand—electricity or rental housing, for example—prices are rising and supplies are dwindling. However troublesome the shortages, though, there are few better or more efficient options for helping the refugees buy basic necessities.

To be sure, cash is no panacea. Not every person will grow his or her income or business with a grant; some recipients will use all the money to pay for immediate needs. The effectiveness of cash-transfer programs are only partly proven, and many unknowns and risks remain. But the evidence is stacking up faster in favor of cash than it is for a lot of the alternatives, and direct cash transfers deserve to shed their reputation of being eccentric. Just as important, donors and the public must hold charitable organizations accountable for the wasteful expenses they regularly incur. The expansion of cash-transfer programs themselves could do the most to bring such costs into clearer focus. And when that happens, the global effort to end poverty will have entered a new and better era.

CHRISTOPHER BLATTMAN is Assistant Professor of Political Science and International Affairs at Columbia University. Follow him on Twitter @cblatts.

PAUL NIEHAUS is Assistant Professor of Economics at the University of California, San Diego, and Co-Founder of GiveDirectly. Follow him on Twitter @Give_Directly.

New World Order

Labor, Capital, and Ideas in the Power Law Economy

Erik Brynjolfsson,
Andrew McAfee,
and Michael Spence   FROM OUR JULY/AUGUST 2014 ISSUE

Robots at the "Hannover Messe" trade fair in Hanover, Germany, April 2014. (Morris Mac Matzen / Courtesy Reuters)

Recent advances in technology have created an increasingly unified global marketplace for labor and capital. The ability of both to flow to their highest-value uses, regardless of their location, is equalizing their prices across the globe. In recent years, this broad factor-price equalization has benefited nations with abundant low-cost labor and those with access to cheap capital. Some have argued that the current era of rapid technological progress serves labor, and some have argued that it serves capital. What both camps have slighted is the fact that technology is not only integrating existing sources of labor and capital but also creating new ones.

Machines are substituting for more types of human labor than ever before. As they replicate themselves, they are also creating more capital. This means that the real winners of the future will not be the providers of cheap labor or the owners of ordinary capital, both of whom will be increasingly squeezed by automation. Fortune will instead favor a third group: those who can innovate and create new products, services, and business models.

The distribution of income for this creative class typically takes the form of a power law, with a small number of winners capturing most of the rewards and a long tail consisting of the rest of the participants. So in the future, ideas will be the real scarce inputs in the world—scarcer than both labor and capital—and the few who provide good ideas will reap huge rewards. Assuring an acceptable standard of living for the rest and building inclusive economies and societies will become increasingly important challenges in the years to come.

LABOR PAINS

Turn over your iPhone and you can read an eight-word business plan that has served Apple well: "Designed by Apple in California. Assembled in China." With a market capitalization of over $500 billion, Apple has become the most valuable company in the world. Variants of this strategy have worked not only for Apple and other large global enterprises but also for medium-sized firms and even "micro-multinationals." More and more companies have been riding the two great forces of our era—technology and globalization—to profits.

Technology has sped globalization forward, dramatically lowering communication and transaction costs and moving the world much closer to a single, large global market for labor, capital, and other inputs to production. Even though labor is not fully mobile, the other factors increasingly are. As a result, the various components of global supply chains can move to labor's location with little friction or cost. About one-third of the goods and services in advanced economies are tradable, and the figure is rising.

And the effect of global competition spills over to the nontradable part of the economy, in both advanced and developing economies.

All of this creates opportunities for not only greater efficiencies and profits but also enormous dislocations. If a worker in China or India can do the same work as one in the United States, then the laws of economics dictate that they will end up earning similar wages (adjusted for some other differences in national productivity). That's good news for overall economic efficiency, for consumers, and for workers in developing countries—but not for workers in developed countries who now face low-cost competition. Research indicates that the tradable sectors of advanced industrial countries have not been net employment generators for two decades. That means job creation now takes place almost exclusively within the large nontradable sector, whose wages are held down by increasing competition from workers displaced from the tradable sector.

Even as the globalization story continues, however, an even bigger one is starting to unfold: the story of automation, including artificial intelligence, robotics, 3-D printing, and so on. And this second story is surpassing the first, with some of its greatest effects destined to hit relatively unskilled workers in developing nations.

Visit a factory in China's Guangdong Province, for example, and you will see thousands of young people working day in and day out on routine, repetitive tasks, such as connecting two parts of a keyboard. Such jobs are rarely, if ever, seen anymore in the United States or the rest of the rich world. But they may not exist for long in China and the rest of the developing world either, for they involve exactly the type of tasks that are easy for robots to do. As intelligent machines become cheaper and more capable, they will increasingly replace human labor, especially in relatively structured environments such as factories and especially for the most routine and repetitive tasks. To put it another way, offshoring is often only a way station on the road to automation.

This will happen even where labor costs are low. Indeed, Foxconn, the Chinese company that assembles iPhones and iPads, employs more than a million low-income workers—but now, it is supplementing and replacing them with a growing army of robots. So after many manufacturing jobs moved from the United States to China, they appear to be vanishing from China as well. (Reliable data on this transition are hard to come by. Official Chinese figures report a decline of 30 million manufacturing jobs since 1996, or 25 percent of the total, even as manufacturing output has soared by over 70 percent, but part of that drop may reflect revisions in the methods of gathering data.) As work stops chasing cheap labor, moreover, it will gravitate toward wherever the final market is, since that will add value by shortening delivery times, reducing inventory costs, and the like.

The growing capabilities of automation threaten one of the most reliable strategies that poor countries have used to attract outside investment: offering low wages to compensate for low productivity and skill levels. And the trend will extend beyond manufacturing. Interactive voice response systems, for example, are reducing the requirement for direct person-to-person interaction, spelling trouble for call centers in the developing world. Similarly, increasingly reliable computer programs will cut into transcription work now often done in the developing world. In more and more domains, the most cost-effective source of "labor" is becoming intelligent and flexible machines as opposed to low-wage humans in other countries.

CAPITAL PUNISHMENT

If cheap, abundant labor is no longer a clear path to economic progress, then what is? One school of thought points to the growing contributions of capital: the physical and intangible assets that combine with labor to produce the goods and services in an economy (think of equipment, buildings, patents, brands, and so on). As the economist Thomas Piketty argues in his best-selling book *Capital in the Twenty-first Century*, capital's share of the economy tends to grow when the rate of return on it is greater than the general rate of economic growth, a condition he predicts for the future. The "capital deepening" of economies that Piketty forecasts will be accelerated further as robots, computers, and software (all of which are forms of capital) increasingly substitute for human workers. Evidence indicates that just such a form of capital-based technological change is taking place in the United States and around the world.

In the past decade, the historically consistent division in the United States between the share of total national income going to labor and that going to physical capital seems to have changed significantly. As the economists Susan Fleck, John Glaser, and Shawn Sprague noted in the U.S. Bureau of Labor Statistics' *Monthly Labor Review* in 2011, "Labor share averaged 64.3 percent from 1947 to 2000. Labor share has declined over the past decade, falling to its lowest point in the third quarter of 2010, 57.8 percent." Recent moves to "re-shore" production from overseas, including Apple's decision to produce its new Mac Pro computer in Texas, will do little to reverse this trend. For in order to be economically viable, these new domestic manufacturing facilities will need to be highly automated.

Other countries are witnessing similar trends. The economists Loukas Karabarbounis and Brent Neiman have documented significant declines in labor's share of GDP in 42 of the 59 countries they studied, including China, India, and Mexico. In describing their findings, Karabarbounis and Neiman are explicit that progress in digital technologies is an important driver of this phenomenon: "The decrease in the relative price of investment goods, often attributed to advances in information technology and the computer age, induced firms to shift away from labor and toward capital. The lower price of investment goods explains roughly half of the observed decline in the labor share."

But if capital's share of national income has been growing, the continuation of such a trend into the future may be in jeopardy as a new challenge to capital emerges—not from a revived labor sector but from an increasingly important unit within its own ranks: digital capital.

In a free market, the biggest premiums go to the scarcest inputs needed for production. In a world where capital such as software and robots can be replicated cheaply, its marginal value will tend to fall, even if more of it is used in the aggregate. And as more capital is added cheaply at the margin, the value of existing capital will actually be driven down. Unlike, say, traditional factories, many types of digital capital can be added extremely cheaply. Software can be duplicated and distributed at almost zero incremental cost. And many elements of computer hardware, governed by variants of Moore's law, get quickly and consistently cheaper over time. Digital capital, in short, is abundant, has low marginal costs, and is increasingly important in almost every industry.

Even as production becomes more capital-intensive, therefore, the rewards earned by capitalists as a group may not necessarily continue to grow relative to labor. The shares will depend on the exact details of the production, distribution, and governance systems.

Most of all, the payoff will depend on which inputs to production are scarcest. If digital technologies create cheap substitutes for a growing set of jobs, then it is not a good time to be a laborer. But if digital technologies also increasingly substitute for capital, then all owners of capital should not expect to earn outsized returns, either.

TECHCRUNCH DISRUPT

What will be the scarcest, and hence the most valuable, resource in what two of us (Erik Brynjolfsson and Andrew McAfee) have called "the second machine age," an era driven by digital technologies and their associated economic characteristics? It will be neither ordinary labor nor ordinary capital but people who can create new ideas and innovations.

Such people have always been economically valuable, of course, and have often profited handsomely from their innovations as a result. But they had to share the returns on their ideas with the labor and capital that were necessary for bringing them into the marketplace. Digital technologies increasingly make both ordinary labor and ordinary capital commodities, and so a greater share of the rewards from ideas will go to the creators, innovators, and entrepreneurs. People with ideas, not workers or investors, will be the scarcest resource.

The most basic model economists use to explain technology's impact treats it as a simple multiplier for everything else, increasing overall productivity evenly for everyone. This model is used in most introductory economics classes and provides the foundation for the common—and, until recently, very sensible—intuition that a rising tide of technological progress will lift all boats equally, making all workers more productive and hence more valuable.

A slightly more complex and realistic model, however, allows for the possibility that technology may not affect all inputs equally but instead favor some more than others. Skill-based technical change, for example, plays to the advantage of more skilled workers relative to less skilled ones, and capital-based technical change favors capital relative to labor. Both of those types of technical change have been important in the past, but increasingly, a third type—what we call superstar-based technical change—is upending the global economy.

Today, it is possible to take many important goods, services, and processes and codify them. Once codified, they can be digitized, and once digitized, they can be replicated. Digital copies can be made at virtually zero cost and transmitted anywhere in the world almost instantaneously, each an exact replica of the original. The combination of these three characteristics—extremely low cost, rapid ubiquity, and perfect fidelity—leads to some weird and wonderful economics. It can create abundance where there had been scarcity, not only for consumer goods, such as music videos, but also for economic inputs, such as certain types of labor and capital.

The returns in such markets typically follow a distinct pattern—a power law, or Pareto curve, in which a small number of players reap a disproportionate share of the rewards. Network effects, whereby a product becomes more valuable the more users it has, can also generate these kinds of winner-take-all or winner-take-most markets. Consider Instagram, the photo-sharing platform, as an example of the economics of the digital, networked economy. The 14 people who created the company didn't need a lot of unskilled human helpers to do so, nor did they need much physical capital. They built a digital product that benefited from network effects, and when it caught on quickly, they were able to sell it after only a year and a half for nearly three-quarters of a billion dollars—ironically, months after the bankruptcy of another photography company, Kodak, that at its peak had employed some 145,000 people and held billions of dollars in capital assets.

Instagram is an extreme example of a more general rule. More often than not, when improvements in digital technologies make it more attractive to digitize a product or process, superstars see a boost in their incomes, whereas second bests, second movers, and latecomers have a harder time competing. The top performers in music, sports, and other areas have also seen their reach and incomes grow since the 1980s, directly or indirectly riding the same trends upward.

But it is not only software and media that are being transformed. Digitization and networks are becoming more pervasive in every industry and function across the economy, from retail and financial services to manufacturing and marketing. That means superstar economics are affecting more goods, services, and people than ever before.

Even top executives have started earning rock-star compensation. In 1990, CEO pay in the United States was, on average, 70 times as large as the salaries of other workers; in 2005, it was 300 times as large. Executive compensation more generally has been going in the same direction globally, albeit with considerable variation from country to country. Many forces are at work here, including tax and policy changes, evolving cultural and organizational norms, and plain luck. But as research by one of us (Brynjolfsson) and Heekyung Kim has shown, a portion of the growth is linked to the greater use of information technology. Technology expands the potential reach, scale, and monitoring capacity of a decision-maker, increasing the value of a good decision-maker by magnifying the potential consequences of his or her choices. Direct management via digital technologies makes a good manager more valuable than in earlier times, when executives had to share control with long chains of subordinates and could affect only a smaller range of activities. Today, the larger the market value of a company, the more compelling the argument for trying to get the very best executives to lead it.

When income is distributed according to a power law, most people will be below the average, and as national economies writ large are increasingly subject to such dynamics, that pattern will play itself out on the national level. And sure enough, the United States today features one of the world's highest levels of real GDP per capita—even as its median income has essentially stagnated for two decades.

PREPARING FOR THE PERMANENT REVOLUTION

The forces at work in the second machine age are powerful, interactive, and complex. It is impossible to look far into the future and predict with any precision what their ultimate impact will be. If individuals, businesses, and governments understand what is going on, however, they can at least try to adjust and adapt.

The United States, for example, stands to win back some business as the second sentence of Apple's eight-word business plan is overturned because its technology and manufacturing operations are once again performed inside U.S. borders. But the first sentence of the plan will become more important than ever, and here, concern, rather than complacency, is in order. For unfortunately, the dynamism and creativity that have made the United States the most innovative nation in the world may be faltering.

Thanks to the ever-onrushing digital revolution, design and innovation have now become part of the tradable sector of the global economy and will face the same sort of competition that has already transformed manufacturing. Leadership in design depends on an educated work force and an entrepreneurial culture, and the traditional American advantage in these areas is declining. Although the United States once led the world in the share of graduates in the work force with at least an associate's degree, it has now fallen to 12th place. And despite the buzz about entrepreneurship in places such as Silicon Valley, data show that since 1996, the number of U.S. start-ups employing more than one person has declined by over 20 percent.

If the trends under discussion are global, their local effects will be shaped, in part, by the social policies and investments that countries choose to make, both in the education sector specifically and in fostering innovation and economic dynamism more generally. For over a century, the U.S. educational system was the envy of the world, with universal K–12 schooling and world-class universities propelling sustained economic growth. But in recent decades, U.S. primary and secondary schooling have become increasingly uneven, with their quality based on neighborhood income levels and often a continued emphasis on rote learning.

Fortunately, the same digital revolution that is transforming product and labor markets can help transform education as well. Online learning can provide students with access to the best teachers, content, and methods regardless of their location, and new data-driven approaches to the field can make it easier to measure students' strengths, weaknesses, and progress. This should create opportunities for personalized learning programs and continuous improvement, using some of the feedback techniques that have already transformed scientific discovery, retail, and manufacturing.

Globalization and technological change may increase the wealth and economic efficiency of nations and the world at large, but they will not work to everybody's advantage, at least in the short to medium term. Ordinary workers, in particular, will continue to bear the brunt of the changes, benefiting as consumers but not necessarily as producers. This means that without further intervention, economic inequality is likely to continue to increase, posing a variety of problems. Unequal incomes can lead to unequal opportunities, depriving nations of access to talent and undermining the social contract. Political power, meanwhile, often follows economic power, in this case undermining democracy.

These challenges can and need to be addressed through the public provision of high-quality basic services, including education, health care, and retirement security. Such services will be crucial for creating genuine equality of opportunity in a rapidly changing economic environment and increasing intergenerational mobility in income, wealth, and future prospects.

As for spurring economic growth in general, there is a near consensus among serious economists about many of the policies that are necessary. The basic strategy is intellectually simple, if politically difficult: boost public-sector investment over the short and medium term while making such investment more efficient and putting in place a fiscal consolidation plan over the longer term. Public investments are known to yield high returns in basic research in health, science, and technology; in education; and in infrastructure spending on roads, airports, public water and sanitation systems, and energy and communications grids. Increased government spending in these areas would boost economic growth now even as it created real wealth for subsequent generations later.

Should the digital revolution continue to be as powerful in the future as it has been in recent years, the structure of the modern economy and the role of work itself may need to be rethought. As a group, our descendants may work fewer hours and live better—but both the work and the rewards could be spread even more unequally, with a variety of unpleasant consequences. Creating sustainable, equitable, and inclusive growth will require more than business as usual. The place to start is with a proper understanding of just how fast and far things are evolving.

ERIK BRYNJOLFSSON is Schussel Family Professor of Management Science at the MIT Sloan School of Management and Co-Founder of MIT's Initiative on the Digital Economy.

ANDREW MCAFEE is a Principal Research Scientist at the MIT Center for Digital Business at the MIT Sloan School of Management and Co-Founder of MIT's Initiative on the Digital Economy.

MICHAEL SPENCE is William R. Berkley Professor in Economics and Business at the NYU Stern School of Business.

America in Decay

The Sources of Political Dysfunction

Francis Fukuyama

FROM OUR SEPTEMBER/
OCTOBER 2014 ISSUE

Man on a mission: a U.S. Forest Service ranger on Mount Silcox, in Montana, 1909. (Corbis / W. J. Lubken)

The creation of the U.S. Forest Service at the turn of the twentieth century was the premier example of American state building during the Progressive Era. Prior to the passage of the Pendleton Act in 1883, public offices in the United States had been allocated by political parties on the basis of patronage. The Forest Service, in contrast, was the prototype of a new model of merit-based bureaucracy. It was staffed with university-educated agronomists and foresters chosen on the basis of competence and technical expertise, and its defining struggle was the successful effort by its initial leader, Gifford Pinchot, to secure bureaucratic autonomy and escape routine interference by Congress. At the time, the idea that forestry professionals, rather than politicians, should manage public lands and handle the department's staffing was revolutionary, but it was vindicated by the service's impressive performance. Several major academic studies have treated its early decades as a classic case of successful public administration.

Today, however, many regard the Forest Service as a highly dysfunctional bureaucracy performing an outmoded mission with the wrong tools. It is still staffed by professional foresters, many highly dedicated to the agency's mission, but it has lost a great deal of the autonomy it won under Pinchot. It operates under multiple and often contradictory mandates from Congress and the courts and costs taxpayers a substantial amount of money while achieving questionable aims. The service's internal decision-making system is often gridlocked, and the high degree of staff morale and cohesion that Pinchot worked so hard to foster has been lost. These days, books are written arguing that the Forest Service ought to be abolished altogether. If the Forest Service's creation exemplified the development of the modern American state, its decline exemplifies that state's decay.

Civil service reform in the late nineteenth century was promoted by academics and activists such as Francis Lieber, Woodrow Wilson, and Frank Goodnow, who believed in the ability of modern natural science to solve human problems. Wilson, like his contemporary Max Weber, distinguished between politics and administration. Politics, he argued, was a domain of final ends, subject to democratic contestation, but administration was a realm of implementation, which could be studied empirically and subjected to scientific analysis.

The belief that public administration could be turned into a science now seems naive and misplaced. But back then, even in advanced countries, governments were run largely by political hacks or corrupt municipal bosses, so it was perfectly reasonable to demand that public officials be selected on the basis of education and merit rather than cronyism. The problem with scientific management is that even the most qualified scientists of the day occasionally get things wrong, and sometimes in a big way. And unfortunately, this is what happened to the Forest Service with regard to what ended up becoming one of its crucial missions, the fighting of forest fires.

Pinchot had created a high-quality agency devoted to one basic goal: managing the sustainable exploitation of forest resources. The Great Idaho Fire of 1910, however, burned some three million acres and killed at least 85 people, and the subsequent political outcry led the Forest Service to focus increasingly not just on timber harvesting but also on wildfire suppression. Yet the early proponents of scientific forestry didn't properly understand the role of fires in woodland ecology. Forest fires are a natural occurrence and serve an important function in maintaining the health of western forests. Shade-intolerant trees, such as ponderosa pines, lodgepole pines, and giant sequoias, require periodic fires to clear areas in which they can regenerate, and once fires were suppressed, these trees were invaded by species such as the Douglas fir. (Lodgepole pines actually require fires to propagate their seeds.) Over the years, many American forests developed high tree densities and huge buildups of dry understory, so that when fires did occur, they became much larger and more destructive.

After catastrophes such as the huge Yellowstone fires in 1988, which ended up burning nearly 800,000 acres in the park and took several months to control, the public began to take notice. Ecologists began criticizing the very objective of fire prevention, and in the mid-1990s, the Forest Service reversed course and officially adopted a "let burn" approach. But years of misguided policies could not simply be erased, since so many forests had become gigantic tinderboxes.

As a result of population growth in the American West, moreover, in the later decades of the twentieth century, many more people began living in areas vulnerable to wildfires. As are people choosing to live on floodplains or on barrier islands, so these individuals were exposing themselves to undue risks that were mitigated by what essentially was government-subsidized insurance. Through their elected representatives, they lobbied hard to make sure the Forest Service and other federal agencies responsible for forest management were given the resources to continue fighting fires that could threaten their property. Under these circumstances, rational cost-benefit analysis proved difficult, and rather than try to justify a decision not to act, the government could easily end up spending $1 million to protect a $100,000 home.

While all this was going on, the original mission of the Forest Service was eroding. Timber harvests in national forests, for example, plunged, from roughly 11 billion to roughly three billion board feet per year in the 1990s alone. This was due partly to the changing economics of the timber industry, but it was also due to a change in national values. With the rise of environmental consciousness, natural forests were increasingly seen as havens to be protected for their own sake, not economic resources to be exploited. And even in terms of economic exploitation, the Forest Service had not been doing a good job. Timber was being marketed at well below the costs of operations; the agency's timber

Mission on the move: fighting flames near Camp Mather, California, August 2013. (Reuters / Max Whittaker)

pricing was inefficient; and as with all government agencies, the Forest Service had an incentive to increase its costs rather than contain them.

The Forest Service's performance deteriorated, in short, because it lost the autonomy it had gained under Pinchot. The problem began with the displacement of a single departmental mission by multiple and potentially conflicting ones. In the middle decades of the twentieth century, firefighting began to displace timber exploitation, but then firefighting itself became controversial and was displaced by conservation. None of the old missions was discarded, however, and each attracted outside interest groups that supported different departmental factions: consumers of timber, homeowners, real estate developers, environmentalists, aspiring firefighters, and so forth. Congress, meanwhile, which had been excluded from the micromanagement of land sales under Pinchot, reinserted itself by issuing various legislative mandates, forcing the Forest Service to pursue several different goals, some of them at odds with one another.

Thus, the small, cohesive agency created by Pinchot and celebrated by scholars slowly evolved into a large, Balkanized one. It became subject to many of the maladies affecting government agencies more generally: its officials came to be more interested in protecting their budgets and jobs than in the efficient performance of their mission. And they clung to old mandates even when both science and the society around them were changing.

The story of the U.S. Forest Service is not an isolated case but representative of a broader trend of political decay; public administration specialists have documented a steady deterioration in the overall quality of American government for more than a generation. In many ways, the U.S. bureaucracy has moved away from the Weberian ideal of an energetic and efficient organization staffed by people chosen for their ability and technical knowledge. The system as a whole is less merit-based: rather than coming from top schools, 45 percent of recent new hires to the federal service are veterans, as mandated by Congress. And a number of surveys of the federal work force paint a depressing picture. According to the scholar Paul Light, "Federal employees appear to be more motivated by compensation than mission, ensnared in careers that cannot compete with business and nonprofits, troubled by the lack of resources to do their jobs, dissatisfied with the rewards for a job well done and the lack of consequences for a job done poorly, and unwilling to trust their own organizations."

WHY INSTITUTIONS DECAY

In his classic work *Political Order in Changing Societies*, the political scientist Samuel Huntington used the term "political decay" to explain political instability in many newly independent countries after World War II. Huntington argued that socioeconomic modernization caused problems for traditional political orders, leading to the mobilization of new social groups whose participation could not be accommodated by existing political institutions. Political decay was caused by the inability of institutions to adapt to changing circumstances. Decay was thus in many ways a condition of political development: the old had to break down in order to make way for the new. But the transitions could be extremely chaotic and violent, and there was no guarantee that the old political institutions would continuously and peacefully adapt to new conditions.

This model is a good starting point for a broader understanding of political decay more generally. Institutions are "stable, valued, recurring patterns of behavior," as Huntington put it, the most important function of which is to facilitate collective action. Without some set of clear and relatively stable rules, human beings would have to renegotiate their interactions at every turn. Such rules are often culturally determined and vary across different societies and eras, but the capacity to create and adhere to them is genetically hard-wired into the human brain. A natural tendency to conformism helps give institutions inertia and is what has allowed human societies to achieve levels of social cooperation unmatched by any other animal species.

The very stability of institutions, however, is also the source of political decay. Institutions are created to meet the demands of specific circumstances, but then circumstances change and institutions fail to adapt. One reason is cognitive: people develop mental models of how the world works and tend to stick to them, even in the face of contradictory evidence. Another reason is group interest: institutions create favored classes of insiders who develop a stake in the status quo and resist pressures to reform.

In theory, democracy, and particularly the Madisonian version of democracy that was enshrined in the U.S. Constitution, should mitigate the problem of such insider capture by preventing the emergence of a dominant faction or elite that can use its political power to tyrannize over the country. It does so by spreading power among a series of competing branches of government and allowing for competition among different interests across a large and diverse country.

But Madisonian democracy frequently fails to perform as advertised. Elite insiders typically have superior access to power and information, which they use to protect their interests. Ordinary voters will not get angry at a corrupt politician if they don't know that money is being stolen in the first place. Cognitive rigidities or beliefs may also prevent social groups from mobilizing in their own interests. For example, in the United States, many working-class voters support candidates promising to lower taxes on the wealthy, despite the fact that such tax cuts will arguably deprive them of important government services.

Furthermore, different groups have different abilities to organize to defend their interests. Sugar producers and corn growers are geographically concentrated and focused on the prices of their products, unlike ordinary consumers or taxpayers, who are dispersed and for whom the prices of these commodities are only a small part of their budgets. Given institutional rules that often favor special interests (such as the fact that Florida and Iowa, where sugar and corn are grown, are electoral swing states), those groups develop an outsized influence over agricultural and trade policy. Similarly, middle-class groups are usually much more willing and able to defend their interests, such as the preservation of the home mortgage tax deduction, than are the poor. This makes such universal entitlements as Social Security or health insurance much easier to defend politically than programs targeting the poor only.

Finally, liberal democracy is almost universally associated with market economies, which tend to produce winners and losers and amplify what James Madison termed the "different and unequal faculties of acquiring property." This type of economic inequality is not in itself a bad thing, insofar as it stimulates innovation and growth and occurs under conditions of equal access to the economic system. It becomes highly problematic, however, when the economic winners seek to convert their wealth into unequal political influence. They can do so by bribing a legislator or a bureaucrat, that is, on a transactional basis, or, what is more damaging, by changing the institutional rules to favor themselves—for example, by closing off competition in markets they already dominate, tilting the playing field ever more steeply in their favor.

Political decay thus occurs when institutions fail to adapt to changing external circumstances, either out of intellectual rigidities or because of the power of incumbent elites to protect their positions and block change. Decay can afflict any type of political system, authoritarian or democratic. And while democratic political systems theoretically have self-correcting mechanisms that allow them to reform, they also open themselves up to decay by legitimating the activities of powerful interest groups that can block needed change.

This is precisely what has been happening in the United States in recent decades, as many of its political institutions have become increasingly dysfunctional. A combination of intellectual rigidity and the power of entrenched political actors is preventing those institutions from being reformed. And there is no guarantee that the situation will change much without a major shock to the political order.

A STATE OF COURTS AND PARTIES

Modern liberal democracies have three branches of government—the executive, the judiciary, and the legislature—corresponding to the three basic categories of political institutions: the state, the rule of law, and democracy. The executive is the branch that uses power to enforce rules and carry out policy; the judiciary and the legislature constrain power and direct it to public purposes. In its institutional priorities, the United States, with its long-standing tradition of distrust of government power, has always emphasized the role of the institutions of constraint—the judiciary and the legislature—over the state. The political scientist Stephen Skowronek has characterized American politics during the nineteenth century as a "state of courts and parties," where government functions that in Europe would have been performed by an executive-branch bureaucracy were performed by judges and elected representatives instead. The creation of a modern, centralized, merit-based bureaucracy capable of exercising jurisdiction over the whole territory of the country began only in the 1880s, and the number of professional civil servants increased slowly up through the New Deal a half century later. These changes came far later and more hesitantly than in countries such as France, Germany, and the United Kingdom.

The shift to a more modern administrative state was accompanied by an enormous growth in the size of government during the middle decades of the twentieth century. Overall levels of both taxes and government spending have not changed very much since the 1970s; despite the backlash against the welfare state that began with President Ronald Reagan's election in 1980, "big government" seems very difficult to dismantle. But the apparently irreversible increase in the scope of government in the twentieth century has masked a large decay in its quality. This is largely because the United States has returned in certain ways to being a "state of courts and parties," that is, one in which the courts and the legislature have usurped many of the proper functions of the executive, making the operation of the government as a whole both incoherent and inefficient.

The story of the courts is one of the steadily increasing judicialization of functions that in other developed democracies are handled by administrative bureaucracies, leading to an explosion of costly litigation, slowness of decision-making, and highly inconsistent enforcement of laws. In the United States today, instead of being constraints on government, courts have become alternative instruments for the expansion of government.

There has been a parallel usurpation by Congress. Interest groups, having lost their ability to corrupt legislators directly through bribery, have found other means of capturing and controlling legislators. These interest groups exercise influence way out of proportion to their place in society, distort both taxes and spending, and raise overall deficit levels by their ability to manipulate the budget in their favor. They also undermine the quality of public administration through the multiple mandates they induce Congress to support.

Both phenomena—the judicialization of administration and the spread of interest-group influence—tend to undermine the trust that people have in government. Distrust of government then perpetuates and feeds on itself. Distrust of executive agencies leads to demands for more legal checks on administration, which reduces the quality and effectiveness of government. At the same time, demand for government services induces Congress to impose new mandates on the executive, which often prove difficult, if not impossible, to fulfill. Both processes lead to a reduction of bureaucratic autonomy, which in turn leads to rigid, rule-bound, uncreative, and incoherent government.

The result is a crisis of representation, in which ordinary citizens feel that their supposedly democratic government no longer truly reflects their interests and is under the control of a variety of shadowy elites. What is ironic and peculiar about this phenomenon is that this crisis of representation has occurred in large part because of reforms designed to make the system more democratic. In fact, these days there is too much law and too much democracy relative to American state capacity.

JUDGES GONE WILD

One of the great turning points in twentieth-century U.S. history was the Supreme Court's 1954 *Brown v. Board of Education* decision overturning the 1896 *Plessy v. Ferguson* case, which had upheld legal segregation. The *Brown* decision was the starting point for the civil rights movement, which succeeded in dismantling the formal barriers to racial equality and guaranteed the rights of African Americans and other minorities. The model of using the courts to enforce new social rules was then followed by many other social movements, from environmental protection and consumer safety to women's rights and gay marriage.

So familiar is this heroic narrative to Americans that they are seldom aware of how peculiar an approach to social change it is. The primary mover in the *Brown* case was the National Association for the Advancement of Colored People, a private voluntary association that filed a class-action suit against the Topeka, Kansas, Board of Education on behalf of a small group of parents and their children. The initiative had to come from private groups, of course, because both the state government and the U.S. Congress were blocked by pro-segregation forces. The NAACP continued to press the case on appeal all the way to the Supreme Court, where it was represented by the future Supreme Court justice Thurgood Marshall. What was arguably one of the most important changes in American public policy came about not because Congress as representative of the American people voted for it but because private individuals litigated through the court system to change the rules. Later changes such as the Civil Rights Act and the Voting Rights Act were the result of congressional action, but even in these cases, the enforcement of national law was left up to the initiative of private parties and carried out by courts.

There is virtually no other liberal democracy that proceeds in this fashion. All European countries have gone through similar changes in the legal status of racial and ethnic minorities, women, and gays in the second half of the twentieth century. But in France, Germany, and the United Kingdom, the same result was achieved not using the courts but through a national justice ministry acting on behalf of a parliamentary majority. The legislative rule change was driven by public pressure from social groups and the media but was carried out by the government itself and not by private parties acting in conjunction with the justice system.

The origins of the U.S. approach lie in the historical sequence by which its three sets of institutions evolved. In countries such as France and Germany, law came first, followed by a modern state, and only later by democracy. In the United States, by contrast, a very deep tradition of English common law came first, followed by democracy, and only later by the development of a modern state. Although the last of these institutions was put into place during the Progressive Era and the New Deal, the American state has always remained weaker and less capable than its European or Asian counterparts. More important, American political culture since the founding has been built around distrust of executive authority.

This history has resulted in what the legal scholar Robert Kagan labels a system of "adversarial legalism." While lawyers have played an outsized role in American public life since the beginning of the republic, their role expanded dramatically during the turbulent years of social change in the 1960s and 1970s. Congress passed more than two dozen major pieces of civil rights and environment legislation in this period, covering issues from product safety to toxic waste cleanup to private pension funds to occupational safety and health. This constituted a huge expansion of the regulatory state, one that businesses and conservatives are fond of complaining about today.

Yet what makes this system so unwieldy is not the level of regulation per se but the highly legalistic way in which it is pursued. Congress mandated the creation of an alphabet soup of new federal agencies, such as the Equal Employment Opportunity Commission, the Environmental Protection Agency, and the Occupational Safety and Health Administration, but it was not willing to cleanly delegate to these bodies the kind of rule-making authority and enforcement power that European or Japanese state institutions enjoy. What it did instead was turn over to the courts the responsibility for monitoring and enforcing the law. Congress deliberately encouraged litigation by expanding standing (that is, who has a right to sue) to an ever-wider circle of parties, many of which were only distantly affected by a particular rule.

The political scientist R. Shep Melnick, for example, has described the way that the federal courts rewrote Title VII of the 1964 Civil Rights Act, "turning a weak law focusing primarily on intentional discrimination into a bold mandate to compensate for past discrimination." Instead of providing a federal bureaucracy with adequate enforcement power, the political scientist Sean Farhang explained, "the key move of Republicans in the Senate . . . was to substantially privatize the prosecutorial function. They made private lawsuits the dominant mode of Title VII enforcement, creating an engine that would, in the years to come, produce levels of private enforcement litigation beyond their imagining." Across the board, private enforcement cases grew in number from less than 100 per year in the late 1960s to 10,000 in the 1980s and over 22,000 by the late 1990s.

Thus, conflicts that in Sweden or Japan would be solved through quiet consultations between interested parties in the bureaucracy are fought out through formal litigation in the U.S. court system. This has a number of unfortunate consequences for public administration, leading to a process characterized, in Farhang's words, by "uncertainty, procedural complexity, redundancy, lack of finality, high transaction costs." By keeping enforcement out of the bureaucracy, it also makes the system far less accountable.

The explosion of opportunities for litigation gave access, and therefore power, to many formerly excluded groups, beginning with African Americans. For this reason, litigation and the right to sue have been jealously guarded by many on the progressive left. But it also entailed large costs in terms of the quality of public policy. Kagan illustrates this with the case of the dredging of Oakland Harbor, in California. During the 1970s, the Port of Oakland initiated plans to dredge the harbor in anticipation

Christopher Blattman and Paul Niehaus

of the new, larger classes of container ships that were then coming into service. The plan, however, had to be approved by a host of federal agencies, including the Army Corps of Engineers, the Fish and Wildlife Service, the National Marine Fisheries Service, and the Environmental Protection Agency, as well as their counterparts in the state of California. A succession of alternative plans for disposing of toxic materials dredged from the harbor were challenged in the courts, and each successive plan entailed prolonged delays and higher costs. The reaction of the Environmental Protection Agency to these lawsuits was to retreat into a defensive crouch and not take action. The final plan to proceed with the dredging was not forthcoming until 1994, at an ultimate cost that was many times the original estimates. A comparable expansion of the Port of Rotterdam, in the Netherlands, was accomplished in a fraction of the time.

Examples such as this can be found across the entire range of activities undertaken by the U.S. government. Many of the travails of the Forest Service can be attributed to the ways in which its judgments could be second-guessed through the court system. This effectively brought to a halt all logging on lands it and the Bureau of Land Management operated in the Pacific Northwest during the early 1990s, as a result of threats to the spotted owl, which was protected under the Endangered Species Act.

When used as an instrument of enforcement, the courts have morphed from constraints on government to mechanisms by which the scope of government has expanded enormously. For example, special-education programs for handicapped and disabled children have mushroomed in size and cost since the mid-1970s as a result of an expansive mandate legislated by Congress in 1974. This mandate was built, however, on earlier findings by federal district courts that special-needs children had rights, which are much harder than mere interests to trade off against other goods or to subject to cost-benefit criteria.

The solution to this problem is not necessarily the one advocated by many conservatives and libertarians, which is to simply eliminate regulation and close down bureaucracies. The ends that government is serving, such as the regulation of toxic waste or environmental protection or special education, are important ones that private markets will not pursue if left to their own devices. Conservatives often fail to see that it is the very distrust of government that leads the American system into a far less efficient court-based approach to regulation than that chosen in democracies with stronger executive branches.

But the attitude of progressives and liberals is equally problematic. They, too, have distrusted bureaucracies, such as the ones that produced segregated school systems in the South or the ones captured by big business, and they have been happy to inject unelected judges into the making of social policy when legislators have proved insufficiently supportive.

A decentralized, legalistic approach to administration dovetails with the other notable feature of the U.S. political system: its openness to the influence of interest groups. Such groups can get their way by suing the government directly. But they have another, even more powerful channel, one that controls significantly more resources: Congress.

LIBERTY AND PRIVILEGE

With the exception of some ambassadorships and top posts in government departments, U.S. political parties are no longer in the business of distributing government offices to loyal political supporters. But the trading of political influence for money has come in through the backdoor, in a form that is perfectly legal and much harder to eradicate. Criminalized bribery is narrowly defined in U.S. law as a transaction in which a politician and a private party explicitly agree on a specific quid pro quo. What is not covered by the law is what biologists call reciprocal altruism, or what an anthropologist might label a gift exchange. In a relationship of reciprocal altruism, one person confers a benefit on another with no explicit expectation that it will buy a return favor. Indeed, if one gives someone a gift and then immediately demands a gift in return, the recipient is likely to feel offended and refuse what is offered. In a gift exchange, the receiver incurs not a legal obligation to provide some specific good or service but rather a moral obligation to return the favor in some way later on. It is this sort of transaction that the U.S. lobbying industry is built around.

Kin selection and reciprocal altruism are two natural modes of human sociability. Modern states create strict rules and incentives to overcome the tendency to favor family and friends, including practices such as civil service examinations, merit qualifications, conflict-of-interest regulations, and antibribery and anticorruption laws. But the force of natural sociability is so strong that it keeps finding a way to penetrate the system.

Over the past half century, the American state has been "repatrimonialized," in much the same way as the Chinese state in the Later Han dynasty, the Mamluk regime in Turkey just before its defeat by the Ottomans, and the French state under the ancien régime were. Rules blocking nepotism are still strong enough to prevent overt favoritism from being a common political feature in contemporary U.S. politics (although it is interesting to note how strong the urge to form political dynasties is, with all of the Kennedys, Bushes, Clintons, and the like). Politicians do not typically reward family members with jobs; what they do is engage in bad behavior on behalf of their families, taking money from interest groups and favors from lobbyists in order to make sure that their children are able to attend elite schools and colleges, for example.

Reciprocal altruism, meanwhile, is rampant in Washington and is the primary channel through which interest groups have succeeded in corrupting government. As the legal scholar Lawrence Lessig points out, interest groups are able to influence members of Congress legally simply by making donations and waiting for unspecified return favors. And sometimes, the legislator is the one initiating the gift exchange, favoring an interest group in the expectation that he will get some sort of benefit from it after leaving office.

The explosion of interest groups and lobbying in Washington has been astonishing, with the number of firms with registered lobbyists rising from 175 in 1971 to roughly 2,500 a decade later, and then to 13,700 lobbyists spending about $3.5 billion by 2009. Some scholars have argued that all this money and activity has not resulted in measurable changes in policy along the lines desired by the lobbyists, implausible as this may seem. But oftentimes, the impact of interest groups and lobbyists is not to stimulate new policies but to make existing legislation much worse than it would otherwise be. The legislative process in the United States has always been much more fragmented than in countries with parliamentary systems and disciplined parties. The welter of congressional committees with overlapping jurisdictions often leads to multiple and conflicting mandates for action. This decentralized legislative process produces incoherent laws and virtually invites involvement by interest groups, which, if not powerful enough to shape overall legislation, can at least protect their specific interests.

For example, the health-care bill pushed by the Obama administration in 2010 turned into something of a monstrosity during the legislative process as a result of all the concessions and side payments that had to be made to interest groups ranging from doctors to insurance companies to the pharmaceutical industry. In other cases, the impact of interest groups was to block legislation harmful to their interests. The simplest and most effective response to the 2008 financial crisis and the hugely unpopular taxpayer bailouts of large banks would have been a law that put a hard cap on the size of financial institutions or a law that dramatically raised capital requirements, which would have had much the same effect. If a cap on size existed, banks taking foolish risks could go bankrupt without triggering a systemic crisis and a government bailout. Like the Depression-era Glass-Steagall Act, such a law could have been written on a couple of sheets of paper. But this possibility was not seriously considered during the congressional deliberations on financial regulation.

What emerged instead was the Dodd-Frank Wall Street Reform and Consumer Protection Act, which, while better than no regulation at all, extended to hundreds of pages of legislation and mandated reams of further detailed rules that will impose huge costs on banks and consumers down the road. Rather than simply capping bank size, it created the Financial Stability Oversight Council, which was assigned the enormous task of assessing and managing institutions posing systemic risks, a move that in the end will still not solve the problem of banks being "too big to fail." Although no one will ever find a smoking gun linking banks' campaign contributions to the votes of specific members of Congress, it defies belief that the banking industry's legions of lobbyists did not have a major impact in preventing the simpler solution of simply breaking up the big banks or subjecting them to stringent capital requirements.

Ordinary Americans express widespread disdain for the impact of interest groups and money on Congress. The perception that the democratic process has been corrupted or hijacked is not an exclusive concern of either end of the political spectrum; both Tea Party Republicans and liberal Democrats believe that interest groups are exercising undue political influence and feathering their own nests. As a result, polls show that trust in Congress has fallen to historically low levels, barely above single digits—and the respondents have a point. Of the old elites in France prior to the Revolution, Alexis de Tocqueville said that they mistook privilege for liberty, that is, they sought protection from state power that applied to them alone and not generally to all citizens. In the contemporary United States, elites speak the language of liberty but are perfectly happy to settle for privilege.

WHAT MADISON GOT WRONG

The economist Mancur Olson made one of the most famous arguments about the malign effects of interest-group politics on economic growth and, ultimately, democracy in his 1982 book *The Rise and Decline of Nations*. Looking particularly at the long-term economic decline of the United Kingdom throughout the twentieth century, he argued that in times of peace and stability, democracies tended to accumulate ever-increasing numbers of interest groups. Instead of pursuing wealth-creating economic activities, these groups used the political system to extract benefits or rents for themselves.

These rents were collectively unproductive and costly to the public as a whole. But the general public had a collective-action problem and could not organize as effectively as, for example, the banking industry or corn producers to protect their interests. The result was the steady diversion of energy to rent-seeking activities over time, a process that could be halted only by a large shock such as a war or a revolution.

This highly negative narrative about interest groups stands in sharp contrast to a much more positive one about the benefits of civil society, or voluntary associations, to the health of democracy. Tocqueville noted in *Democracy in America* that Americans had a strong propensity to organize private associations, which he argued were schools for democracy because they taught private individuals the skills of coming together for public purposes. Individuals by themselves were weak; only by coming together for common purposes could they, among other things, resist tyrannical government. This perspective was carried forward in the late twentieth century by scholars such as Robert Putnam, who argued that this very propensity to organize—"social capital"—was both good for democracy and endangered.

Madison himself had a relatively benign view of interest groups. Even if one did not approve of the ends that a particular group was seeking, he argued, the diversity of groups over a large country would be sufficient to prevent domination by any one of them. As the political scientist Theodore Lowi has noted, "pluralist" political theory in the mid-twentieth century concurred with Madison: the cacophony of interest groups would collectively interact to produce a public interest, just as competition in a free market would provide public benefit through individuals' following their narrow self-interests. There were no grounds for the government to regulate this process, since there was no higher authority that could define a public interest standing above the narrow concerns of interest groups. The Supreme Court in its *Buckley v. Valeo* and *Citizens United* decisions, which struck down certain limits on campaign spending by groups, was in effect affirming the benign interpretation of what Lowi has labeled "interest group liberalism."

How can these diametrically opposed narratives be reconciled? The most obvious way is to try to distinguish a "good" civil society organization from a "bad" interest group. The former could be said to be driven by passions, the latter by interests. A civil society organization might be a nonprofit such as a church group seeking to build houses for the poor or else a lobbying organization promoting a public policy it believed to be in the public interest, such as the protection of coastal habitats. An interest group might be a lobbying firm representing the tobacco industry or large banks, whose objective was to maximize the profits of the companies supporting it.

Unfortunately, this distinction does not hold up to theoretical scrutiny. Just because a group proclaims that it is acting in the public interest does not mean that it is actually doing so. For example, a medical advocacy group that wanted more dollars allocated to combating a particular disease might actually distort public priorities by diverting funds from more widespread and damaging diseases, simply because it is better at public relations. And because an interest group is self-interested doesn't mean that its claims are illegitimate or that it does not have a right to be represented within the political system. If a poorly-thought-out regulation would seriously damage the interests of an industry and its workers, the relevant interest group has a right to make that known to Congress. In fact, such lobbyists are often some of the most important sources of information about the consequences of government action.

The most salient argument against interest-group pluralism has to do with distorted representation. In his 1960 book *The Semisovereign People*, E. E. Schattschneider argued that the actual practice of democracy in the United States had nothing to do with its popular image as a government "of the people, by the people, for the people." He noted that political outcomes seldom correspond with popular preferences, that there is a very low level of participation and political awareness, and that real decisions are taken by much smaller groups of organized interests. A similar argument is buried in Olson's framework, since Olson notes that not all groups are equally capable of organizing for collective action. The interest groups that contend for the attention of Congress represent not the whole American people but the best-organized and (what often amounts to the same thing) most richly endowed parts of American society. This tends to work against the interests of the unorganized, who are often poor, poorly educated, or otherwise marginalized.

The political scientist Morris Fiorina has provided substantial evidence that what he labels the American "political class" is far more polarized than the American people themselves. But the majorities supporting middle-of-the-road positions do not feel very passionately about them, and they are largely unorganized. This means that politics is defined by well-organized activists, whether in the parties and Congress, the media, or in lobbying and interest groups. The sum of these activist groups does not yield a compromise position; it leads instead to polarization and deadlocked politics.

There is a further problem with the pluralistic view, which sees the public interest as nothing more than the aggregation of individual private interests: it undermines the possibility of deliberation and the process by which individual preferences are shaped by dialogue and communication. Both classical Athenian democracy and the New England town hall meetings celebrated by Tocqueville were cases in which citizens spoke directly to one another about the common interests of their communities. It is easy to idealize these instances of small-scale democracy, or to minimize the real differences that exist in large societies. But as any organizer of focus groups will tell you, people's views on highly emotional subjects, from immigration to abortion to drugs, will change just 30 minutes into a face-to-face discussion with people of differing views, provided that they are all given the same information and ground rules that enforce civility. One of the problems of pluralism, then, is the assumption that interests are fixed and that the role of the legislator is simply to act as a transmission belt for them, rather than having his own views that can be shaped by deliberation.

Christopher Blattman and Paul Niehaus

THE RISE OF VETOCRACY

The U.S. Constitution protects individual liberties through a complex system of checks and balances that were deliberately designed by the founders to constrain the power of the state. American government arose in the context of a revolution against British monarchical authority and drew on even deeper wellsprings of resistance to the king during the English Civil War. Intense distrust of government and a reliance on the spontaneous activities of dispersed individuals have been hallmarks of American politics ever since.

As Huntington pointed out, in the U.S. constitutional system, powers are not so much functionally divided as replicated across the branches, leading to periodic usurpations of one branch by another and conflicts over which branch should predominate. Federalism often does not cleanly delegate specific powers to the appropriate level of government; rather, it duplicates them at multiple levels, giving federal, state, and local authorities jurisdiction over, for example, toxic waste disposal. Under such a system of redundant and non-hierarchical authority, different parts of the government are easily able to block one another. In conjunction with the general judicialization of politics and the widespread influence of interest groups, the result is an unbalanced form of government that undermines the prospects of necessary collective action—something that might more appropriately be called "vetocracy."

The two dominant American political parties have become more ideologically polarized than at any time since the late nineteenth century. There has been a partisan geographic sorting, with virtually the entire South moving from Democratic to Republican and Republicans becoming virtually extinct in the Northeast. Since the breakdown of the New Deal coalition and the end of the Democrats' hegemony in Congress in the 1980s, the two parties have become more evenly balanced and have repeatedly exchanged control over the presidency and Congress. This higher degree of partisan competition, in turn, along with liberalized campaign-finance guidelines, has fueled an arms race between the parties for funding and has undermined personal comity between them. The parties have also increased their homogeneity through their control, in most states, over redistricting, which allows them to gerrymander voting districts to increase their chances of reelection. The spread of primaries, meanwhile, has put the choice of party candidates into the hands of the relatively small number of activists who turn out for these elections.

Polarization is not the end of the story, however. Democratic political systems are not supposed to end conflict; rather, they are meant to peacefully resolve and mitigate it through agreed-on rules. A good political system is one that encourages the emergence of political outcomes representing the interests of as large a part of the population as possible. But when polarization confronts the United States' Madisonian check-and-balance political system, the result is particularly devastating.

Democracies must balance the need to allow full opportunities for political participation for all, on the one hand, and the need to get things done, on the other. Ideally, democratic decisions would be taken by consensus, with every member of the community consenting. This is what typically happens in families, and how band- and tribal-level societies often make decisions. The efficiency of consensual decision-making, however, deteriorates rapidly as groups become larger and more diverse, and so for most groups, decisions are made not by consensus but with the consent of some subset of the population. The smaller the percentage of the group necessary to take a decision, the more easily and efficiently it can be made, but at the expense of long-run buy-in.

Even systems of majority rule deviate from an ideal democratic procedure, since they can disenfranchise nearly half the population. Indeed, under a plurality, or "first past the post," electoral system, decisions can be taken for the whole community by a minority of voters. Systems such as these are adopted not on the basis of any deep principle of justice but rather as an expedient that allows decisions of some sort to be made. Democracies also create various other mechanisms, such as cloture rules (enabling the cutting off of debate), rules restricting the ability of legislators to offer amendments, and so-called reversionary rules, which allow for action in the event that a legislature can't come to agreement.

The delegation of powers to different political actors enables them to block action by the whole body. The U.S. political system has far more of these checks and balances, or what political scientists call "veto points," than other contemporary democracies, raising the costs of collective action and in some cases make it impossible altogether. In earlier periods of U.S. history, when one party or another was dominant, this system served to moderate the will of the majority and force it to pay greater attention to minorities than it otherwise might have. But in the more evenly balanced, highly competitive party system that has arisen since the 1980s, it has become a formula for gridlock.

By contrast, the so-called Westminster system, which evolved in England in the years following the Glorious Revolution of 1688, is one of the most decisive in the democratic world because, in its pure form, it has very few veto points. British citizens have one large, formal check on government, their ability to periodically elect Parliament. (The tradition of free media in the United Kingdom is another important informal check.) In all other respects, however, the system concentrates, rather than diffuses, power. The pure Westminster system has only a single, all-powerful legislative chamber—no separate presidency, no powerful upper house, no written constitution and therefore no judicial review, and no federalism or constitutionally mandated devolution of powers to localities. It has a plurality voting system that, along with strong party discipline, tends to produce a two-party system and strong parliamentary majorities. The British equivalent of the cloture rule requires only a simple majority of the members of Parliament to be present to call the question; American-style filibustering is not allowed. The parliamentary majority chooses a government with strong executive powers, and when it makes a legislative decision, it generally cannot be stymied by courts, states, municipalities, or other bodies. This is why the British system is often described as a "democratic dictatorship."

For all its concentrated powers, the Westminster system nonetheless remains fundamentally democratic, because if voters don't like the government it produces, they can vote it out of office. In fact, with a vote of no confidence, they can do so immediately, without waiting for the end of a presidential term. This means that governments are more sensitive to perceptions of their general performance than to the needs of particular interest groups or lobbies.

The Westminster system produces stronger governments than those in the United States, as can be seen by comparing their budget processes. In the United Kingdom, national budgets are drawn up by professional civil servants acting under instructions from the cabinet and the prime minister. The budget is then presented by the chancellor of the exchequer to the House of Commons, which votes to approve it in a single up-or-down vote, usually within a week or two.

In the United States, by contrast, Congress has primary authority over the budget. Presidents make initial proposals, but these are largely aspirational documents that do not determine what eventually emerges. The executive branch's Office of Management and Budget has no formal powers over the budget, acting as simply one more lobbying organization supporting the president's preferences. The budget works its way through a complex set of committees over a period of months, and what finally emerges for ratification by the two houses of Congress is the product of innumerable deals struck with individual members to secure their support—since with no party discipline, the congressional leadership cannot compel members to support its preferences.

The openness and never-ending character of the U.S. budget process gives lobbyists and interest groups multiple points at which to exercise influence. In most European parliamentary systems, it would make no sense for an interest group to lobby an individual member of parliament, since the rules of party discipline would give that legislator little or no influence over the party leadership's position. In the United States, by contrast, an influential committee chairmanship confers enormous powers to modify legislation and therefore becomes the target of enormous lobbying activity.

Of the challenges facing developed democracies, one of the most important is the problem of the unsustainability of their existing welfare-state commitments. The existing social contracts underlying contemporary welfare states were negotiated several generations ago, when birthrates were higher, lifespans were shorter, and economic growth rates were robust. The availability of finance has allowed all modern democracies to keep pushing this problem into the future, but at some point, the underlying demographic reality will set in.

These problems are not insuperable. The debt-to-GDP ratios of both the United Kingdom and the United States coming out of World War II were higher than they are today. Sweden, Finland, and other Scandinavian countries found their large welfare states in crisis during the 1990s and were able to make adjustments to their tax and spending levels. Australia succeeded in eliminating almost all its external debt, even prior to the huge resource boom of the early years of this century. But dealing with these problems requires a healthy, well-functioning political system, which the United States does not currently have. Congress has abdicated one of its most basic responsibilities, having failed to follow its own rules for the orderly passing of budgets several years in a row now.

The classic Westminster system no longer exists anywhere in the world, including the United Kingdom itself, as that country has gradually adopted more checks and balances. Nonetheless, the United Kingdom still has far fewer veto points than does the United States, as do most parliamentary systems in Europe and Asia. (Certain Latin American countries, having copied the U.S. presidential system in the nineteenth century, have similar problems with gridlock and politicized administration.)

Budgeting is not the only aspect of government that is handled differently in the United States. In parliamentary systems, a great deal of legislation is formulated by the executive branch with heavy technocratic input from the permanent civil service. Ministries are accountable to parliament, and hence ultimately to voters, through the ministers who head them, but this type of hierarchical system can take a longer-term strategic view and produce much more coherent legislation.

Such a system is utterly foreign to the political culture in Washington, where Congress jealously guards its right to legislate—even though the often incoherent product is what helps produce a large, sprawling, and less accountable government. Congress' multiple committees frequently produce duplicate and overlapping programs or create several agencies with similar purposes. The Pentagon, for example, operates under nearly 500 mandates to report annually to Congress on various issues. These never expire, and executing them consumes huge amounts of time and energy. Congress has created about 50 separate programs for worker retraining and 82 separate projects to improve teacher quality.

Financial-sector regulation is split between the Federal Reserve, the Treasury Department, the Securities and Exchange Commission, the Federal Deposit Insurance Corporation, the National Credit Union Administration, the Commodity Futures Trading Commission, the Federal Housing Finance Agency, and a host of state attorneys general who have decided to take on the banking sector. The federal agencies are overseen by different congressional committees, which are loath to give up their turf to a more coherent and unified regulator. This system was easy to game so as to bring about the deregulation of the financial sector in the late 1990s; re-regulating it after the recent financial crisis has proved much more difficult.

CONGRESSIONAL DELEGATION

Vetocracy is only half the story of the U.S. political system. In other respects, Congress delegates huge powers to the executive branch, which allow the latter to operate rapidly and sometimes with a very low degree of accountability. Such areas of delegation include the Federal Reserve, the intelligence agencies, the military, and a host of quasi-independent commissions and regulatory agencies that together constitute the huge administrative state that emerged during the Progressive Era and the New Deal.

While many American libertarians and conservatives would like to abolish these agencies altogether, it is hard to see how it would be possible to govern properly under modern circumstances without them. The United States today has a huge, complex national economy, situated in a globalized world economy that moves with extraordinary speed. During the acute phase of the financial crisis that unfolded after the collapse of Lehman Brothers in September 2008, the Federal Reserve and the Treasury Department had to make massive decisions overnight, decisions that involved flooding markets with trillions of dollars of liquidity, propping up individual banks, and imposing new regulations. The severity of the crisis led Congress to appropriate $700 billion for the Troubled Asset Relief Program largely on the say-so of the Bush administration. There has been a lot of second-guessing of individual decisions made during this period, but the idea that such a crisis could have been managed by any other branch of government is ludicrous. The same applies to national security issues, where the president is in effect tasked with making decisions on how to respond to nuclear and terrorist threats that potentially affect the lives of millions of Americans. It is for this reason that Alexander Hamilton, in *The Federalist Papers*, no. 70, spoke of the need for "energy in the executive."

There is intense populist distrust of elite institutions in the United States, together with calls to abolish them (as in the case of the Federal Reserve) or make them more transparent. Ironically, however, polls show the highest degree of approval for precisely those institutions, such as the military or NASA, that are the least subject to immediate democratic oversight. Part of the reason they are admired is that they can actually get things done. By contrast, the most democratic institution, the House of Representatives, receives disastrously low levels of approval, and Congress more broadly is regarded (not inaccurately) as a talking shop where partisan games prevent almost anything useful from happening.

In full perspective, therefore, the U.S. political system presents a complex picture in which checks and balances excessively constrain decision-making on the part of majorities, but in which there are also many instances of potentially dangerous delegations of authority to poorly accountable institutions. One major problem is that these delegations are seldom made cleanly. Congress frequently fails in its duty to provide clear legislative guidance on how a particular agency is to perform its task, leaving it up to the agency itself to write its own mandate. In doing so, Congress hopes that if things don't work out, the courts will step in to correct the abuses. Excessive delegation and vetocracy thus become intertwined.

In a parliamentary system, the majority party or coalition controls the government directly; members of parliament become ministers who have the authority to change the rules of the bureaucracies they control. Parliamentary systems can be blocked if parties are excessively fragmented and coalitions unstable, as has been the case frequently in Italy. But once a parliamentary majority has been established, there is a relatively straight-forward delegation of authority to an executive agency.

Such delegations are harder to achieve, however, in a presidential system. The obvious solution to a legislature's inability to act is to transfer more authority to the separately elected executive. Latin American countries with presidential systems have been notorious for gridlock and ineffective legislatures and have often cut through the maze by granting presidents emergency powers—which, in turn, has often led to other kinds of abuses. Under conditions of divided government, when the party controlling one or both houses of Congress is different from the one controlling the presidency, strengthening the executive at the expense of Congress becomes a matter of partisan politics. Delegating more authority to President Barack Obama is the last thing that House Republicans want to do today.

In many respects, the American system of checks and balances compares unfavorably with parliamentary systems when it comes to the ability to balance the need for strong state action with law and accountability. Parliamentary systems tend not to judicialize administration to nearly the same extent; they have proliferated government agencies less, they write more coherent legislation, and they are less subject to interest-group influence. Germany, the Netherlands, and the Scandinavian countries, in particular, have been able to sustain higher levels of trust in government, which makes public administration less adversarial, more consensual, and better able to adapt to changing conditions of globalization. (High-trust arrangements, however, tend to work best in relatively small, homogeneous societies, and those in these countries have been showing signs of strain as their societies have become more diverse as a result of immigration and cultural change.)

The picture looks a bit different for the EU as a whole. Recent decades have seen a large increase in the number and sophistication of lobbying groups in Europe, for example. These days, corporations, trade associations, and environmental, consumer, and labor rights groups all operate at both national and EU-wide levels. And with the shift of policymaking away from national capitals to Brussels, the European system as a whole is beginning to resemble that of the United States in depressing ways. Europe's individual parliamentary systems may allow for fewer veto points than the U.S. system of checks and balances, but with the addition of a large European layer, many more veto points have been added. This means that European interest groups are increasingly able to venue shop: if they cannot get favorable treatment at the national level, they can go to Brussels, or vice versa. The growth of the EU has also Americanized Europe with respect to the role of the judiciary. Although European judges remain more reluctant than their U.S. counterparts to insert themselves into political matters, the new structure of European jurisprudence, with its multiple and overlapping levels, has increased, rather than decreased, the number of judicial vetoes in the system.

NO WAY OUT

The U.S. political system has decayed over time because its traditional system of checks and balances has deepened and become increasingly rigid. In an environment of sharp political polarization, this decentralized system is less and less able to represent majority interests and gives excessive representation to the views of interest groups and activist organizations that collectively do not add up to a sovereign American people.

This is not the first time that the U.S. political system has been polarized and indecisive. In the middle decades of the nineteenth century, it could not make up its mind about the extension of slavery to the territories, and in the later decades of the century, it couldn't decide if the country was a fundamentally agrarian society or an industrial one. The Madisonian system of checks and balances and the clientelistic, party-driven political system that emerged in the nineteenth century were adequate for governing an isolated, largely agrarian country. They could not, however, resolve the acute political crisis produced by the question of the extension of slavery, nor deal with a continental-scale economy increasingly knit together by new transportation and communications technologies.

Today, once again, the United States is trapped by its political institutions. Because Americans distrust government, they are generally unwilling to delegate to it the authority to make decisions, as happens in other democracies. Instead, Congress mandates complex rules that reduce the government's autonomy and cause decision-making to be slow and expensive. The government then doesn't perform well, which confirms people's lack of trust in it. Under these circumstances, they are reluctant to pay higher taxes, which they feel the government will simply waste. But without appropriate resources, the government can't function properly, again creating a self-fulfilling prophecy.

Two obstacles stand in the way of reversing the trend toward decay. The first is a matter of politics. Many political actors in the United States recognize that the system isn't working well but nonetheless have strong interests in keeping things as they are. Neither political party has an incentive to cut itself off from access to interest-group money, and the interest groups don't want a system in which money won't buy influence. As happened in the 1880s, a reform coalition has to emerge that unites groups without a stake in the current system. But achieving collective action among such out-groups is very difficult; they need leadership and a clear agenda, neither of which is currently present.

The second problem is a matter of ideas. The traditional American solution to perceived governmental dysfunction has been to try to expand democratic participation and transparency. This happened at a national level in the 1970s, for example, as reformers pushed for more open primaries, greater citizen access to the courts, and round-the-clock media coverage of Congress, even as states such as California expanded their use of ballot initiatives to get around unresponsive government. But as the political scientist Bruce Cain has pointed out, most citizens have neither the time, nor the background, nor the inclination to grapple with complex public policy issues; expanding participation has simply paved the way for well-organized groups of activists to gain more power. The obvious solution to this problem would be to roll back some of the would-be democratizing reforms, but no one dares suggest that what the country needs is a bit less participation and transparency.

The depressing bottom line is that given how self-reinforcing the country's political malaise is, and how unlikely the prospects for constructive incremental reform are, the decay of American politics will probably continue until some external shock comes along to catalyze a true reform coalition and galvanize it into action.

FRANCIS FUKUYAMA is a Senior Fellow at the Center on Democracy, Development, and the Rule of Law at Stanford University. This essay is adapted from his forthcoming book, Political Order and Political Decay: From the French Revolution to the Present (Farrar, Straus and Giroux, 2014). Copyright © 2014 by Francis Fukuyama.

Pitchfork Politics

The Populist Threat to Liberal Democracy

Yascha Mounk

FROM OUR SEPTEMBER/
OCTOBER 2014 ISSUE

Flare-up: demonstrating at the European Parliament, in Brussels, April 2013. (Reuters / Francois Lenoir)

Since Roman times, virtually every type of government that holds competitive elections has experienced some form of populism—some attempt by ambitious politicians to mobilize the masses in opposition to an establishment they depict as corrupt or self-serving. From Tiberius Gracchus and the *populares* of the Roman Senate, to the champions of the *popolo* in Machiavelli's sixteenth-century Florence, to the Jacobins in Paris in the late eighteenth century, to the Jacksonian Democrats who stormed nineteenth-century Washington—all based their attempts at mass mobilization on appeals to the simplicity and goodness of ordinary people. By the mid-twentieth century, populism had become a common feature of democracy.

But then, during an extended period of spectacular economic growth stretching roughly from the aftermath of World War II to the late 1970s, the political establishments of most Western democracies managed to banish their populist rivals to the innocuous fringes of political discourse. On the right, populists occasionally made incursions at the local or regional level but inevitably failed to gain traction in national elections. On the left, the countercultural protest movements of the 1960s and 1970s challenged the status quo but didn't secure institutional representation until their radicalism had subsided.

As the political scientists Seymour Martin Lipset and Stein Rokkan famously observed, during the postwar years, the party structures of North America and western Europe were "frozen" to an unprecedented degree. Between 1960 and 1990, the parties represented in the parliaments of Amsterdam, Copenhagen, Ottawa, Paris, Rome, Stockholm, Vienna, and Washington barely changed. For a few decades, Western political establishments held such a firm grip on power that most observers stopped noticing just how remarkable that stability was compared to the historical norm.

Yet beginning in the 1990s, a new crop of populists began a steady rise. Over the past two decades, populist movements in Europe and the United States have uprooted traditional party structures and forced ideas long regarded as extremist or unsavory onto the political agenda. The influence of populists has been especially striking in the past few months. In May, Euroskeptical and far-right parties demonstrated unprecedented strength in elections to the European Parliament, even topping the polls in France and the United Kingdom. Meanwhile, in the United States, the Tea Party has sparked a civil war within the Republican Party: the most recent casualty was the House majority leader, Eric Cantor, an influential party power broker who was defeated in a primary election in June by a previously obscure archconservative challenger. The movement is now poised to make major advances in November's midterm elections and will likely be able to hold Congress hostage with its obstructionist tactics for the foreseeable future.

Members of the Western political establishments have explained away this populist wave by pointing to recent events: the financial crisis of 2008 and the Great Recession that followed, they say, account for the growing impatience with the status quo. But that interpretation underestimates the significance of these electoral shifts. Far from reflecting a temporary crisis, the rise of populism stems from a set of long-term challenges that have diminished the ability of democratic governments to satisfy their citizens. These problems, including a long-term stagnation in living standards and deep crises of national identity, will not go away anytime soon— not even if the economies of the Western democracies experience an unforeseen boom in the coming years. The fact is that the past two decades have represented not a populist moment but rather a populist turn—one that will exert significant influence on policy and public opinion for decades to come.

To avoid the serious damage that populists could inflict on democracy, political establishments on both sides of the Atlantic must find a way to channel populist passions for good. To do so, they need to give voice to the justified grievances that fuel populism while convincing voters that the simple solutions offered up by the populists are bound to fail.

NO MERE BLIP

Perhaps the most visible sign of populism's rebirth is the rise of the Tea Party in the United States. The movement first exploded onto the American political scene in 2009. It was initially driven by alarm over Barack Obama's decisive victory in the presidential election of 2008 and by an intense hostility to the health-care reform Obama advocated. But the movement has since broadened its mission into a frontal assault on "big government." Its targets now include not only Democrats but also any Republican whom Tea Party purists consider too moderate. Thanks to its success in radicalizing the Republican mainstream, the Tea Party has now gained so much influence in the House of Representatives that it can exert an effective veto over the entire legislative machinery of the United States.

Populists are well on their way toward holding similar power on the other side of the Atlantic. In countries across Europe, populists of all stripes have transformed domestic politics in recent decades and now threaten the very existence of the EU. In Austria during the 1990s, Jörg Haider, an ultraconservative nationalist, won millions of sympathizers with denunciations of immigrants and thinly veiled nostalgia for the Third Reich. During the following decade, in the Netherlands, Pim Fortuyn gained a loyal following by warning that Muslim immigrants were undermining liberal Dutch traditions.

More recently, in Italy, the Five Star Movement, a party founded just a few years ago by Beppe Grillo, a former comedian, attracted the third-largest share of the vote in national elections last year with a platform grounded in Grillo's demand that "the political caste go fuck itself." In the United Kingdom, the UK Independence Party won the largest share of British votes in May's elections for the European Parliament by fusing a radical rejection of the EU with inflammatory rhetoric about immigrants from eastern Europe. It was the first time in over a century that a British party other than Labour or the Conservatives triumphed in a national election.

Members of the European establishment have reassured themselves with the belief that these populist successes will start to fizzle once the economic effects of the Great Recession and the euro crisis subside. But although political scientists have tried to prove the hypothesis that recessions or spikes in the unemployment rate have a direct influence on the strength of populist parties, most such studies have come up inconclusive. In some countries and during some time periods, moments of acute economic crisis have coincided with a strong showing by populist movements. But just as often, populists have stagnated or even lost support during recessions. As the Dutch political scientist Cas Mudde has pointed out, right-wing populists in Europe did as well in national elections between 2005 and 2008, before the euro crisis began, as they did in the years of acute economic turmoil, from 2009 to 2013. Traumatic as it was, the Great Recession did not bring about an obvious inflection point: the growth in the political strength of populist parties began during the relatively prosperous 1990s and has continued at a fast but steady pace since then.

IDENTITY CRISIS

If short-term fluctuations in economic factors cannot explain the rise of populism, its underlying causes must operate on a longer time scale. And indeed, there do seem to be two fundamental developments that match the timeline of the populist rise and help explain the particular shape populist politics have taken in recent decades: a decline in living standards from one generation to the next and the perceived threat to national identity posed by immigration and the growth of supranational organizations.

The liberal democracies of the West have always been subject to the ups and downs of markets. But for all the extreme booms and recessions they have experienced, one crucial economic fact has remained remarkably constant: except for during brief moments of extreme crisis, the average citizen of a Western democracy has, since the start of the Industrial Revolution, enjoyed a higher standard of living than his or her parents. The typical citizen could expect to have more money, to live longer, and to spend a greater portion of his or her life at leisure. According to an extensive body of research pioneered by the economists Thomas Piketty and Emmanuel Saez, that is no longer the case. In most developed democracies, the median income has remained stagnant over the past 25 years: in the United States, the Census Bureau reported a lower median household income in 2012 than in 1989.

As political scientists such as Jacob Hacker and sociologists such as Ulrich Beck have shown, this loss of income has been compounded by a concurrent loss of security. Average citizens don't just make less money today than they did a generation ago; they are also a lot less certain about their future incomes and their degree of protection against new forms of financial and social risk. It is little wonder, then, that so many citizens not only suffer from a strong sense of economic decline but also are growing increasingly convinced that the political establishment has failed them.

During this period of economic decline, citizens of affluent democracies have also had to deal with new challenges to their national identities. In the wake of the ethnic cleansings and mass deportations of the first half of the twentieth century, most European countries became highly homogeneous. Even when decolonization and the economic boom of the 1950s and 1960s began to attract massive numbers of immigrants to Europe, the influx did not pose a real threat to national identity, since most European governments told their citizens that the recent arrivals were merely temporary visitors who would willingly return home once they had taken advantage of short-term economic opportunities.

But that promise began to ring hollow when, in the decades that followed, millions of immigrants gained the right to remain in their adoptive countries and started to demand that they be accepted as full members of the nation. Many Europeans found that prospect unacceptable: even as official definitions of membership in a European nation became more inclusive, some continued to insist that only those who shared the history and ethnicity of the majority population counted as true Germans, or Italians, or Swedes. Populists have been adept at exploiting these rising tensions, promising to protect the interests of "true" members of the nation from minorities with whom political elites are supposedly in cahoots.

Newcomers to the United States and their families have had an easier time gaining acceptance as "true" Americans, since the country has long defined itself as a nation of immigrants. But American populists, too, have been able to capitalize on a sense of a crisis in national identity. The influx of millions of illegal immigrants has allowed Tea Partiers to claim that the country has lost control of its borders. In some quarters, this has stoked larger fears about rapid changes in the country's cultural and demographic mix: while most Americans of European descent are willing to accept that U.S. citizens come from all kinds of ethnic and cultural backgrounds, some are less willing to countenance the potential end of white dominance over U.S. politics and popular culture. They don't see themselves in figures such as Obama or Supreme Court Justice Sonia Sotomayor, and the ascent of people of color to some of the country's highest political offices only heightens some white Americans' perception that Washington has become distant and alien.

SILENT MAJORITIES

A skeptic might counter that the populist parties currently on the rise don't share enough common goals to be considered part of a unitary movement. But the rising populist parties on both sides of the Atlantic and within Europe are linked not by a set of specific policy proposals but rather by a shared set of core concerns, expressed in a language of outrage against the status quo and the political elites who maintain it.

Populists give voice to such resentment with a repertoire of strikingly similar slogans and tropes. An election manifesto published recently by the UK Independence Party promises to "stand up for local people and local communities against the politicians of the old parties." Marine Le Pen, the leader of France's National Front, complains that "the French, in effect, are no longer consulted on the big questions facing them, from immigration to sovereignty, precisely because the globalized elites who govern us no longer want to hear us talk." Meanwhile, in the United States, the 2008 Republican vice-presidential candidate and conservative commentator Sarah Palin has said that "the best of America is in these small towns . . . and in these wonderful little pockets of what I call the real America," implicitly contrasting "pro-America areas of this great nation" with other parts of the country that are presumably less patriotic. The local color varies, but the overarching themes remain the same.

Indeed, the rhetoric of antiestablishment populism has so suffused Western political discourse in recent years that its most common expressions have become clichés. Although the specifics vary, the populists all argue that current policies favor a minority at the cost of the majority. They all claim that elites, through formal mechanisms or social pressure, censor certain kinds of political speech. The reason for this censorship, they all insinuate, is that the political establishment wants to stop the majority from finding out what the minority is really like and to what extent that minority is being favored by current policies. Now, at long last, the populists proclaim, somebody willing to stand up for the people has arrived on the political scene and will fight for the silent majority by enacting policies that favor them.

ENEMIES OF THE PEOPLE

Despite the similarities among all populists, the word "populist" is a neutral description: not every populist movement has to be bad for democracy. Whether a particular movement poses a threat depends on how it plugs concrete values into the broad populist framework. Populists claim that they serve the neglected interests of the silent majority by standing up against a corrupt establishment that collaborates with some undeserving minority. But how, exactly, would populists serve those interests? And might they not be tempted to repress or mistreat the minority they so eagerly attack?

Those concerns are especially relevant when considering right-wing populists, who believe that minority groups are coddled and overprivileged, diverting much-needed resources from the silent, suffering majority: claims that, most of the time, are simply untrue. In both North America and Europe, for example, supposedly privileged ethnic minorities lag behind the majority in terms of income, life expectancy, and a host of other social indicators, in good part because, as sociological studies have consistently shown, they face serious discrimination in education, the workplace, and the housing market. Given this mismatch between rhetoric and reality, if populists win greater power, they are likely to compound existing injustices and inequalities by giving more to the discontented majority and by taking from minorities that already have less, in both material and social terms, than they deserve.

Most right-wing populists fall into one of four basic categories. Perhaps the most common of these is the national chauvinists, who claim that political elites are insufficiently proud of their country, apologize too readily for the nation's past sins, and too enthusiastically celebrate religious or ethnic minorities.

In Europe, national chauvinism has fueled a number of populist parties, such as Austria's Freedom Party, Hungary's Jobbik, and Greece's Golden Dawn. Even in Germany, where fierce nationalism has long been scorned owing to the country's Nazi past, Thilo Sarrazin, a former Bundesbank board member turned populist polemicist, has won a devoted following by invoking national-chauvinist themes. In 2010, Sarrazin published a runaway bestseller in which he argued that Turkish immigrants to Germany were simply less intelligent than ethnic Germans, in part due to inbreeding. "Whole clans have a long tradition of incest, and correspondingly many disabilities," Sarrazin wrote. "But that topic is greeted with deathly silence. Otherwise, some people might have the idea that genetic factors explain why parts of the Turkish population flunk out of German schools."

A slightly different strand of right-wing thinking, best termed "populist traditionalism," emphasizes the preservation of conventional lifestyles that most citizens supposedly favor. Although many traditionalists also display nationalist or xenophobic tendencies, the main out-groups they fear are internal to the nation itself: intellectuals, aesthetes, homosexuals, and anyone else too elitist to partake in the homespun, innocent pursuits of ordinary folks. Recently, populist traditionalism has enjoyed a surprising resurgence in western Europe, embraced by political parties such as the Finns Party—which promotes a specifically Christian "Finnish identity"—as well as by those grass-roots groups that have brought millions of people out onto the streets of France to protest same-sex marriage.

Traditionalism of this kind is, of course, familiar in the United States, where it has long represented the political core of the religious right—and, to a certain extent, has come to guide the Tea Party movement. But the Tea Party is best understood as an example of a third strain of populism: the antistatist variety. Most populists lament that the state has been led astray by a snooty establishment in bed with immigrants, minorities, atheists, and intellectuals. But they also believe that government has an important role to play in providing for the well-being of its country's citizens. Antistatist populists, on the other hand, see the state itself as the greatest threat to their liberty and their lifestyle, and they wish to be as free as possible from its corrupting influence. As the Republican senator Rand Paul, invoking Ronald Reagan, said in a response to Obama's 2013 State of the Union address that was sponsored by Tea Party groups, "government is not the answer to the problem; government is the problem."

In Europe, antistatism takes the form of Euroskepticism, the belief that the ever-growing power of Brussels-based "Eurocrats" threatens the freedoms of ordinary people in EU member states. As Nigel Farage, the leader of the UK Independence Party, told the president of the European Council during a speech at the European Parliament: "I have no doubt in your intention to be the quiet assassin of European democracy and of the European nation-states." Le Pen has railed against the EU as a "European Soviet Union" and has vowed to prevent it "from grabbing everything with its paws and from extending its tentacles."

A fourth and final set of right-wing populists has ingeniously distanced itself from nationalism, traditionalism, and antistatism by casting its members as defenders of liberal values. In the United States, alarmist propaganda about "creeping sharia"—a stealth campaign allegedly seeking to impose Islamic law in the United States—usually comes from conservatives positioning themselves as defenders of Christian values. By contrast, the kind of Islamophobia that has gained traction in many parts of Europe dresses up similar prejudices as a defense of liberalism. This strain of populism warns that Muslim immigrants and political elites who "appease" them threaten other citizens' freedom to live as they choose. As Fortuyn, the openly gay Dutch politician who was an early spokesperson for liberal Islamophobia, said, "I consider [Islam] a backward culture. I have traveled much in the world. And wherever Islam rules, it's just terrible. . . . Then, look at the Netherlands. In what country could an electoral leader of such a large movement as mine be openly homosexual?"

Inspired by this line of attack, liberal Islamophobes have cropped up throughout France, Germany, the Scandinavian countries—and even Quebec—in the past decade. Insincere though these Islamophobes' invocations of liberalism might be, their ability to cloak their prejudice in the respectable—even noble—language of tolerance makes this group the most dangerous of today's populist movements.

WELFARE FAREWELL

Unlike the New Left, whose countercultural critiques shaped the populism of the 1960s and 1970s, the left-wing populists currently enjoying a revival in Western democracies concentrate on economic issues. Unlike many of their counterparts on the right, whose platforms are based on inflated or invented threats, they tend to focus on very real problems: government and corporate corruption, growing economic inequality, declining social mobility, and the stagnation of living standards. The most visible embodiment of such thinking has been the Occupy Wall Street movement, which rallied around the "99 percent" of people struggling under the thumb of the superrich one percent. A similar form of economic populism animates protest parties in Europe, including Greece's Syriza and Italy's Five Star Movement, both of which have ferociously defended the traditional welfare state and rejected the austerity measures imposed by Athens and Rome—often at the behest of Brussels or Berlin—in the wake of the euro crisis.

These economic populists are right to point out that contemporary democracies are far from flawless. Left to its own devices, capitalist democracy has a tendency to put more power in the hands of the already powerful and more wealth in the hands of the already wealthy. To counterbalance this gradual erosion of economic and political justice, democracies need occasional eruptions of popular anger. In that sense, left-wing populism can be an important corrective to the self-serving temptations to which any elite is likely to succumb over time.

Although the problems that alarm them are genuine, however, left-wing populists, like the right-leaning cohort, cross into fantasy when it comes to solutions—mostly because they underestimate just how deep the roots of the contemporary economic malaise run. They blame entrenched elites for widespread poverty and advance the myth that the fight for economic justice can be won simply by standing up to the big banks (in the United States), or to Berlin (in Europe), or to the World Trade Organization (in both places). If only national governments were allowed to get on with the straightforward business of redistributing wealth and expanding welfare programs, they suggest, the economic lots of ordinary citizens would quickly improve.

But the reality is that many of the problems left-wing populists point out have arisen out of large-scale forces, such as technological innovation, demographic changes, and economic globalization. The rise of digital technologies and increasingly well-educated work forces in Africa, Asia, and Latin America, for example, has reduced global demand for North American and western European labor. Similarly, public pension systems are under pressure not solely because politicians lack the will to finance them properly but also because Western societies are rapidly aging: in 1960, Italy's population had a median age of 31.2; by 2020, it is projected to be 46.2.

Economic populists falsely believe that taking entrenched interests down a peg would be enough to return to the golden days of the recent past. But saving the generous welfare states of North America and western Europe will require a new approach, not a dogged defense of the unsustainable status quo. In denying this messy reality, left-wing populists are just as misguided as their right-wing counterparts.

PASSION WITHOUT PANDER

Over the course of their long history, democracies have been opposed by large swaths of their own citizenries, nostalgic for monarchy, feudalism, or even authoritarian rule. Democratic countries have been deeply divided along ethnic, religious, and linguistic lines. They have torn themselves apart over land reform, found themselves dominated by populists and demagogues, and descended into civil war. And yet when most Westerners hear the word "democracy" today, what they picture is a political atmosphere that is respectful, predictable, and a little staid—a system in which a small number of long-standing political parties alternate in government on a semiregular basis, resulting in reasonably moderate changes to public policy.

Most people are, of course, painfully aware that the politics of today's democracies no longer look much like this; they are more fractured, chaotic, and unpredictable than they were as little as three decades ago. But the period of time during which most Western democracies were essentially stable was extremely short. Indeed, some democracies, such as Italy, have always been dysfunctional. In others, such as the United States, even calm periods were punctuated by moments of lunacy, such as the witchhunts of the McCarthy era or President Richard Nixon's blatant disregard for the rules of the democratic game.

For those who wish to usher in a new period of relative democratic stability, the challenge will be to harness the passion of the populists to the cause of reinvigorating governance, but without helping them kindle the flames of an antidemocratic revolt. In the realm of economic policy, this means addressing the generational decline in living standards that has provided populists with such fertile ground. The leaders of affluent democracies must commit themselves to two goals that are often assumed to conflict: wealth redistribution and economic modernization. Only decisive political action, including a more serious attempt to tax wealth, can ensure that future economic growth will benefit the lower and middle classes as well as the rich. But first, governments have to create the conditions for growth. Especially in southern and western Europe, politicians will have to take deeply unpopular steps, including raising the retirement age and loosening labor regulations. This combination of reform and redistribution will not be easy to pull off. But a new generation of ambitious politicians, including Italy's prime minister, Matteo Renzi, is beginning to win support for painful economic reforms by giving voice to populist frustrations and rallying voters around the goal of redistribution.

An even harder task for establishment politicians will be acknowledging and responding to the widespread sense of a crisis in national identity without pandering to xenophobic populism or dismantling much-needed international institutions. The best strategy is to appeal to nationalist sentiments but reject any suggestion that minorities are less than full members of the nation. That shouldn't prove too hard in the United States, which has a relatively strong tradition of nonethnic nationalism. But mainstream parties in Europe will have a tougher time, since ethnic conceptions of nationhood are more deeply ingrained there than in the United States. Indeed, European politicians might find it impossible to accommodate such sentiments without giving up on the liberal vision of a multiethnic society—a cure for populism that would be worse than the disease.

By contrast, Europe's establishment parties could take some easy steps to allay populist fears about the EU. A promising start would be to renounce their long-standing commitment to an "ever-closer union," an aspiration that makes it all too easy for populists to claim that EU bureaucrats will not rest until they have dismantled Europe's nation-states. By promising a specific endpoint to the process of integration, European leaders could inoculate themselves against the charge that they are weak on sovereignty while protecting the main achievements of the EU, such as the free movement of goods and people.

Whether these suggestions would suffice to halt the populist advance is, of course, far from certain. The extraordinary stability of postwar democracy rested on exceptional economic and demographic trends that have now run their course. Restoring that kind of stability will be an uphill battle. Even if establishment politicians do everything right over the coming decades, the threat posed by populism is here to stay for the foreseeable future.

YASCHA MOUNK is the author of Stranger in My Own Country: A Jewish Family in Modern Germany. He is a Ph.D. candidate in Harvard University's Government Department and a Fellow at the New America Foundation.

Why the Ukraine Crisis Is the West's Fault

The Liberal Delusions That Provoked Putin

John J. Mearsheimer

FROM OUR SEPTEMBER/
OCTOBER 2014 ISSUE

A man takes a picture as he stands on a Soviet-style star re-touched with blue paint so that it resembles the Ukrainian flag, Moscow, August 20, 2014. (Maxim Shemetov / Courtesy Reuters)

According to the prevailing wisdom in the West, the Ukraine crisis can be blamed almost entirely on Russian aggression. Russian President Vladimir Putin, the argument goes, annexed Crimea out of a long-standing desire to resuscitate the Soviet empire, and he may eventually go after the rest of Ukraine, as well as other countries in eastern Europe. In this view, the ouster of Ukrainian President Viktor Yanukovych in February 2014 merely provided a pretext for Putin's decision to order Russian forces to seize part of Ukraine.

But this account is wrong: the United States and its European allies share most of the responsibility for the crisis. The taproot of the trouble is NATO enlargement, the central element of a larger strategy to move Ukraine out of Russia's orbit and integrate it into the West. At the same time, the EU's expansion eastward and the West's backing of the pro-democracy movement in Ukraine—beginning with the Orange Revolution in 2004—were critical elements, too. Since the mid-1990s, Russian leaders have adamantly opposed NATO enlargement, and in recent years, they have made it clear that they would not stand by while their strategically important neighbor turned into a Western bastion. For Putin, the illegal overthrow of Ukraine's democratically elected and pro-Russian president—which he rightly labeled a "coup"—was the final straw. He responded by taking Crimea, a peninsula he feared would host a NATO naval base, and working to destabilize Ukraine until it abandoned its efforts to join the West.

Putin's pushback should have come as no surprise. After all, the West had been moving into Russia's backyard and threatening its core strategic interests, a point Putin made emphatically and repeatedly. Elites in the United States and Europe have been blindsided by events only because they subscribe to a flawed view of international politics. They tend to believe that the logic of realism holds little relevance in the twenty-first century and that Europe can be kept whole and free on the basis of such liberal principles as the rule of law, economic interdependence, and democracy.

But this grand scheme went awry in Ukraine. The crisis there shows that realpolitik remains relevant—and states that ignore it do so at their own peril. U.S. and European leaders blundered in attempting to turn Ukraine into a Western stronghold on Russia's border. Now that the consequences have been laid bare, it would be an even greater mistake to continue this misbegotten policy.

THE WESTERN AFFRONT

As the Cold War came to a close, Soviet leaders preferred that U.S. forces remain in Europe and NATO stay intact, an arrangement they thought would keep a reunified Germany pacified. But they and their Russian successors did not want NATO to grow any larger and assumed that Western diplomats understood their concerns. The Clinton administration evidently thought otherwise, and in the mid-1990s, it began pushing for NATO to expand.

The first round of enlargement took place in 1999 and brought in the Czech Republic, Hungary, and Poland. The second occurred in 2004; it included Bulgaria, Estonia, Latvia, Lithuania, Romania, Slovakia, and Slovenia. Moscow complained bitterly from the start. During NATO's 1995 bombing campaign against the Bosnian Serbs, for example, Russian President Boris Yeltsin said, "This is the first sign of what could happen when NATO comes right up to the Russian Federation's borders. . . . The flame of war could burst out across the whole of Europe." But the Russians were too weak at the time to derail NATO's eastward movement—which, at any rate, did not look so threatening, since none of the new members shared a border with Russia, save for the tiny Baltic countries.

Then NATO began looking further east. At its April 2008 summit in Bucharest, the alliance considered admitting Georgia and Ukraine. The George W. Bush administration supported doing so, but France and Germany opposed the move for fear that it would unduly antagonize Russia. In the end, NATO's members reached a compromise: the alliance did not begin the formal process leading to membership, but it issued a statement endorsing the aspirations of Georgia and Ukraine and boldly declaring, "These countries will become members of NATO."

Moscow, however, did not see the outcome as much of a compromise. Alexander Grushko, then Russia's deputy foreign minister, said, "Georgia's and Ukraine's membership in the alliance is a huge strategic mistake which would have most serious consequences for pan-European security." Putin maintained that admitting those two countries to NATO would represent a "direct threat" to Russia. One Russian newspaper reported that Putin, while speaking with Bush, "very transparently hinted that if Ukraine was accepted into NATO, it would cease to exist."

Russia's invasion of Georgia in August 2008 should have dispelled any remaining doubts about Putin's determination to prevent Georgia and Ukraine from joining NATO. Georgian President Mikheil Saakashvili, who was deeply committed to bringing his country into NATO, had decided in the summer of 2008 to reincorporate two separatist regions, Abkhazia and South Ossetia. But Putin sought to keep Georgia weak and divided—and out of NATO. After fighting broke out between the Georgian government and South Ossetian separatists, Russian forces took control of Abkhazia and South Ossetia. Moscow had made its point. Yet despite this clear warning, NATO never publicly abandoned its goal of bringing Georgia and Ukraine into the alliance. And NATO expansion continued marching forward, with Albania and Croatia becoming members in 2009.

The EU, too, has been marching eastward. In May 2008, it unveiled its Eastern Partnership initiative, a program to foster prosperity in such countries as Ukraine and integrate them into the EU economy. Not surprisingly, Russian leaders view the plan as hostile to their country's interests. This past February, before Yanukovych was forced from office, Russian Foreign Minister Sergey Lavrov accused the EU of trying to create a "sphere of influence" in eastern Europe. In the eyes of Russian leaders, EU expansion is a stalking horse for NATO expansion.

The West's final tool for peeling Kiev away from Moscow has been its efforts to spread Western values and promote democracy in Ukraine and other post-Soviet states, a plan that often entails funding pro-Western individuals and organizations. Victoria Nuland, the U.S. assistant secretary of state for European and Eurasian affairs, estimated in December 2013 that the United States had invested more than $5 billion since 1991 to help Ukraine achieve "the future it deserves." As part of that effort, the U.S. government has bankrolled the National Endowment for Democracy. The nonprofit foundation has funded more than 60 projects aimed at promoting civil society in Ukraine, and the NED's president, Carl Gershman, has called that country "the biggest prize."

After Yanukovych won Ukraine's presidential election in February 2010, the NED decided he was undermining its goals, and so it stepped up its efforts to support the opposition and strengthen the country's democratic institutions.

When Russian leaders look at Western social engineering in Ukraine, they worry that their country might be next. And such fears are hardly groundless. In September 2013, Gershman wrote in *The Washington Post*, "Ukraine's choice to join Europe will accelerate the demise of the ideology of Russian imperialism that Putin represents." He added: "Russians, too, face a choice, and Putin may find himself on the losing end not just in the near abroad but within Russia itself."

CREATING A CRISIS

The West's triple package of policies—NATO enlargement, EU expansion, and democracy promotion—added fuel to a fire waiting to ignite. The spark came in November 2013, when Yanukovych rejected a major economic deal he had been negotiating with the EU and decided to accept a $15 billion Russian counteroffer instead. That decision gave rise to antigovernment demonstrations that escalated over the following three months and that by mid-February had led to the deaths of some one hundred protesters. Western emissaries hurriedly flew to Kiev to resolve the crisis. On February 21, the government and the opposition struck a deal that allowed Yanukovych to stay in power until new elections were held. But it immediately fell apart, and Yanukovych fled to Russia the next day. The new government in Kiev was pro-Western and anti-Russian to the core, and it contained four high-ranking members who could legitimately be labeled neofascists.

Although the full extent of U.S. involvement has not yet come to light, it is clear that Washington backed the coup. Nuland and Republican Senator John McCain participated in antigovernment demonstrations, and Geoffrey Pyatt, the U.S. ambassador to Ukraine, proclaimed after Yanukovych's toppling that it was "a day for the history books." As a leaked telephone recording revealed,

Nuland had advocated regime change and wanted the Ukrainian politician Arseniy Yatsenyuk to become prime minister in the new government, which he did. No wonder Russians of all persuasions think the West played a role in Yanukovych's ouster.

For Putin, the time to act against Ukraine and the West had arrived. Shortly after February 22, he ordered Russian forces to take Crimea from Ukraine, and soon after that, he incorporated it into Russia. The task proved relatively easy, thanks to the thousands of Russian troops already stationed at a naval base in the Crimean port of Sevastopol. Crimea also made for an easy target since ethnic Russians compose roughly 60 percent of its population. Most of them wanted out of Ukraine.

Next, Putin put massive pressure on the new government in Kiev to discourage it from siding with the West against Moscow, making it clear that he would wreck Ukraine as a functioning state before he would allow it to become a Western stronghold on Russia's doorstep. Toward that end, he has provided advisers, arms, and diplomatic support to the Russian separatists in eastern Ukraine, who are pushing the country toward civil war. He has massed a large army on the Ukrainian border, threatening to invade if the government cracks down on the rebels. And he has sharply raised the price of the natural gas Russia sells to Ukraine and demanded payment for past exports. Putin is playing hardball.

THE DIAGNOSIS

Putin's actions should be easy to comprehend. A huge expanse of flat land that Napoleonic France, imperial Germany, and Nazi Germany all crossed to strike at Russia itself, Ukraine serves as a buffer state of enormous strategic importance to Russia. No Russian leader would tolerate a military alliance that was Moscow's mortal enemy until recently moving into Ukraine. Nor would any Russian leader stand idly by while the West helped install a government there that was determined to integrate Ukraine into the West.

Washington may not like Moscow's position, but it should understand the logic behind it. This is Geopolitics 101: great powers are always sensitive to potential threats near their home territory. After all, the United States does not tolerate distant great powers deploying military forces anywhere in the Western Hemisphere, much less on its borders. Imagine the outrage in Washington if China built an impressive military alliance and tried to include Canada and Mexico in it. Logic aside, Russian leaders have told their Western counterparts on many occasions that they consider NATO expansion into Georgia and Ukraine unacceptable, along with any effort to turn those countries against Russia—a message that the 2008 Russian-Georgian war also made crystal clear.

Officials from the United States and its European allies contend that they tried hard to assuage Russian fears and that Moscow should understand that NATO has no designs on Russia. In addition to continually denying that its expansion was aimed at containing Russia, the alliance has never permanently deployed military forces in its new member states. In 2002, it even created a body called the NATO-Russia Council in an effort to foster cooperation. To further mollify Russia, the United States announced in 2009 that it would deploy its new missile defense system on warships in European waters, at least initially, rather than on Czech or Polish territory. But none of these measures worked; the Russians remained steadfastly opposed to NATO enlargement, especially into Georgia and Ukraine. And it is the Russians, not the West, who ultimately get to decide what counts as a threat to them.

To understand why the West, especially the United States, failed to understand that its Ukraine policy was laying the groundwork for a major clash with Russia, one must go back to the mid-1990s, when the Clinton administration began advocating NATO expansion. Pundits advanced a variety of arguments for and against enlargement, but there was no consensus on what to do. Most eastern European émigrés in the United States and their relatives, for example, strongly supported expansion, because they wanted NATO to protect such countries as Hungary and Poland. A few realists also favored the policy because they thought Russia still needed to be contained.

But most realists opposed expansion, in the belief that a declining great power with an aging population and a one-dimensional economy did not in fact need to be contained. And they feared that enlargement would only give Moscow an incentive to cause trouble in eastern Europe. The U.S. diplomat George Kennan articulated this perspective in a 1998 interview, shortly after the U.S. Senate approved the first round of NATO expansion. "I think the Russians will gradually react quite adversely and it will affect their policies," he said. "I think it is a tragic mistake. There was no reason for this whatsoever. No one was threatening anyone else."

Most liberals, on the other hand, favored enlargement, including many key members of the Clinton administration. They believed that the end of the Cold War had fundamentally transformed international politics and that a new, postnational order had replaced the realist logic that used to govern Europe. The United States was not only the "indispensable nation," as Secretary of State Madeleine Albright put it; it was also a benign hegemon and thus unlikely to be viewed as a threat in Moscow. The aim, in essence, was to make the entire continent look like western Europe.

And so the United States and its allies sought to promote democracy in the countries of eastern Europe, increase economic interdependence among them, and embed them in international institutions. Having won the debate in the United States, liberals had little difficulty convincing their European allies to support NATO enlargement. After all, given the EU's past achievements, Europeans were even more wedded than Americans to the idea that geopolitics no longer mattered and that an all-inclusive liberal order could maintain peace in Europe.

So thoroughly did liberals come to dominate the discourse about European security during the first decade of this century that even as the alliance adopted an open-door policy of growth, NATO expansion faced little realist opposition. The liberal worldview is now accepted dogma among U.S. officials. In March, for example, President Barack Obama delivered a speech about Ukraine in which he talked repeatedly about "the ideals" that motivate Western policy and how those ideals "have often been threatened by an older, more traditional view of power." Secretary of State John Kerry's response to the Crimea crisis reflected this same perspective: "You just don't in the twenty-first century behave in nineteenth-century fashion by invading another country on completely trumped-up pretext."

In essence, the two sides have been operating with different playbooks: Putin and his compatriots have been thinking and acting according to realist dictates, whereas their Western counterparts have been adhering to liberal ideas about international politics. The result is that the United States and its allies unknowingly provoked a major crisis over Ukraine.

BLAME GAME

In that same 1998 interview, Kennan predicted that NATO expansion would provoke a crisis, after which the proponents of expansion would "say that we always told you that is how the Russians are." As if on cue, most Western officials have portrayed Putin as the real culprit in the Ukraine predicament. In March, according to *The New York Times*, German Chancellor Angela Merkel implied that Putin was irrational, telling Obama that he was "in another world." Although Putin no doubt has autocratic tendencies, no evidence supports the charge that he is mentally unbalanced. On the contrary: he is a first-class strategist who should be feared and respected by anyone challenging him on foreign policy.

Other analysts allege, more plausibly, that Putin regrets the demise of the Soviet Union and is determined to reverse it by expanding Russia's borders. According to this interpretation, Putin, having taken Crimea, is now testing the waters to see if the time is right to conquer Ukraine, or at least its eastern part, and he will eventually behave aggressively toward other countries in Russia's neighborhood. For some in this camp, Putin represents a modern-day Adolf Hitler, and striking any kind of deal with him would repeat the mistake of Munich. Thus, NATO must admit Georgia and Ukraine to contain Russia before it dominates its neighbors and threatens western Europe.

This argument falls apart on close inspection. If Putin were committed to creating a greater Russia, signs of his intentions would almost certainly have arisen before February 22. But there is virtually no evidence that he was bent on taking Crimea, much less any other territory in Ukraine, before that date. Even Western leaders who supported NATO expansion were not doing so out of a fear that Russia was about to use military force. Putin's actions in Crimea took them by complete surprise and appear to have been a spontaneous reaction to Yanukovych's ouster. Right afterward, even Putin said he opposed Crimean secession, before quickly changing his mind.

Besides, even if it wanted to, Russia lacks the capability to easily conquer and annex eastern Ukraine, much less the entire country. Roughly 15 million people—one-third of Ukraine's population— live between the Dnieper River, which bisects the country, and the Russian border. An overwhelming majority of those people want to remain part of Ukraine and would surely resist a Russian occupation. Furthermore, Russia's mediocre army, which shows few signs of turning into a modern Wehrmacht, would have little chance of pacifying all of Ukraine. Moscow is also poorly positioned to pay for a costly occupation; its weak economy would suffer even more in the face of the resulting sanctions.

But even if Russia did boast a powerful military machine and an impressive economy, it would still probably prove unable to successfully occupy Ukraine. One need only consider the Soviet and U.S. experiences in Afghanistan, the U.S. experiences in Vietnam and Iraq, and the Russian experience in Chechnya to be reminded that military occupations usually end badly. Putin surely understands that trying to subdue Ukraine would be like swallowing a porcupine. His response to events there has been defensive, not offensive.

A WAY OUT

Given that most Western leaders continue to deny that Putin's behavior might be motivated by legitimate security concerns, it is unsurprising that they have tried to modify it by doubling down on their existing policies and have punished Russia to deter further aggression. Although Kerry has maintained that "all options are on the table," neither the United States nor its NATO allies are prepared to use force to defend Ukraine. The West is relying instead on economic sanctions to coerce Russia into ending its support for the insurrection in eastern Ukraine. In July, the United States and the EU put in place their third round of limited sanctions, targeting mainly high-level individuals closely tied to the Russian government and some high-profile banks, energy companies, and defense firms. They also threatened to unleash another, tougher round of sanctions, aimed at whole sectors of the Russian economy.

Such measures will have little effect. Harsh sanctions are likely off the table anyway; western European countries, especially Germany, have resisted imposing them for fear that Russia might retaliate and cause serious economic damage within the EU. But even if the United States could convince its allies to enact tough measures, Putin would probably not alter his decision-making. History shows that countries will absorb enormous amounts of punishment in order to protect their core strategic interests. There is no reason to think Russia represents an exception to this rule.

Western leaders have also clung to the provocative policies that precipitated the crisis in the first place. In April, U.S. Vice President Joseph Biden met with Ukrainian legislators and told them, "This is a second opportunity to make good on the original promise made by the Orange Revolution." John Brennan, the director of the CIA, did not help things when, that same month, he visited Kiev on a trip the White House said was aimed at improving security cooperation with the Ukrainian government.

The EU, meanwhile, has continued to push its Eastern Partnership. In March, José Manuel Barroso, the president of the European Commission, summarized EU thinking on Ukraine, saying, "We have a debt, a duty of solidarity with that country, and we will work to have them as close as possible to us." And sure enough, on

June 27, the EU and Ukraine signed the economic agreement that Yanukovych had fatefully rejected seven months earlier. Also in June, at a meeting of NATO members' foreign ministers, it was agreed that the alliance would remain open to new members, although the foreign ministers refrained from mentioning Ukraine by name. "No third country has a veto over NATO enlargement," announced Anders Fogh Rasmussen, NATO's secretary-general. The foreign ministers also agreed to support various measures to improve Ukraine's military capabilities in such areas as command and control, logistics, and cyberdefense. Russian leaders have naturally recoiled at these actions; the West's response to the crisis will only make a bad situation worse.

There is a solution to the crisis in Ukraine, however—although it would require the West to think about the country in a fundamentally new way. The United States and its allies should abandon their plan to westernize Ukraine and instead aim to make it a neutral buffer between NATO and Russia, akin to Austria's position during the Cold War. Western leaders should acknowledge that Ukraine matters so much to Putin that they cannot support an anti-Russian regime there. This would not mean that a future Ukrainian government would have to be pro-Russian or anti-NATO. On the contrary, the goal should be a sovereign Ukraine that falls in neither the Russian nor the Western camp.

To achieve this end, the United States and its allies should publicly rule out NATO's expansion into both Georgia and Ukraine. The West should also help fashion an economic rescue plan for Ukraine funded jointly by the EU, the International Monetary Fund, Russia, and the United States—a proposal that Moscow should welcome, given its interest in having a prosperous and stable Ukraine on its western flank. And the West should considerably limit its social-engineering efforts inside Ukraine. It is time to put an end to Western support for another Orange Revolution. Nevertheless, U.S. and European leaders should encourage Ukraine to respect minority rights, especially the language rights of its Russian speakers.

Some may argue that changing policy toward Ukraine at this late date would seriously damage U.S. credibility around the world. There would undoubtedly be certain costs, but the costs of continuing a misguided strategy would be much greater. Furthermore, other countries are likely to respect a state that learns from its mistakes and ultimately devises a policy that deals effectively with the problem at hand. That option is clearly open to the United States.

One also hears the claim that Ukraine has the right to determine whom it wants to ally with and the Russians have no right to prevent Kiev from joining the West. This is a dangerous way for Ukraine to think about its foreign policy choices. The sad truth is that might often makes right when great-power politics are at play. Abstract rights such as self-determination are largely meaningless when powerful states get into brawls with weaker states. Did Cuba have the right to form a military alliance with the Soviet Union during the Cold War? The United States certainly did not think so, and the Russians think the same way about Ukraine joining the West. It is in Ukraine's interest to understand these facts of life and tread carefully when dealing with its more powerful neighbor.

Even if one rejects this analysis, however, and believes that Ukraine has the right to petition to join the EU and NATO, the fact remains that the United States and its European allies have the right to reject these requests. There is no reason that the West has to accommodate Ukraine if it is bent on pursuing a wrong-headed foreign policy, especially if its defense is not a vital interest. Indulging the dreams of some Ukrainians is not worth the animosity and strife it will cause, especially for the Ukrainian people.

Of course, some analysts might concede that NATO handled relations with Ukraine poorly and yet still maintain that Russia constitutes an enemy that will only grow more formidable over time—and that the West therefore has no choice but to continue its present policy. But this viewpoint is badly mistaken. Russia is a declining power, and it will only get weaker with time. Even if Russia were a rising power, moreover, it would still make no sense to incorporate Ukraine into NATO. The reason is simple: the United States and its European allies do not consider Ukraine to be a core strategic interest, as their unwillingness to use military force to come to its aid has proved. It would therefore be the height of folly to create a new NATO member that the other members have no intention of defending. NATO has expanded in the past because liberals assumed the alliance would never have to honor its new security guarantees, but Russia's recent power play shows that granting Ukraine NATO membership could put Russia and the West on a collision course.

Sticking with the current policy would also complicate Western relations with Moscow on other issues. The United States needs Russia's assistance to withdraw U.S. equipment from Afghanistan through Russian territory, reach a nuclear agreement with Iran, and stabilize the situation in Syria. In fact, Moscow has helped Washington on all three of these issues in the past; in the summer of 2013, it was Putin who pulled Obama's chestnuts out of the fire by forging the deal under which Syria agreed to relinquish its chemical weapons, thereby avoiding the U.S. military strike that Obama had threatened. The United States will also someday need Russia's help containing a rising China. Current U.S. policy, however, is only driving Moscow and Beijing closer together.

The United States and its European allies now face a choice on Ukraine. They can continue their current policy, which will exacerbate hostilities with Russia and devastate Ukraine in the process—a scenario in which everyone would come out a loser. Or they can switch gears and work to create a prosperous but neutral Ukraine, one that does not threaten Russia and allows the West to repair its relations with Moscow. With that approach, all sides would win.

JOHN J. MEARSHEIMER is R. Wendell Harrison Distinguished Service Professor of Political Science at the University of Chicago.

The Unraveling

How to Respond to a Disordered World

Richard N. Haass

FROM OUR NOVEMBER/
DECEMBER 2014 ISSUE

(vistavision / Flickr)

In his classic *The Anarchical Society*, the scholar Hedley Bull argued that there was a perennial tension in the world between forces of order and forces of disorder, with the details of the balance between them defining each era's particular character. Sources of order include actors committed to existing international rules and arrangements and to a process for modifying them; sources of disorder include actors who reject those rules and arrangements in principle and feel free to ignore or undermine them. The balance can also be affected by global trends, to varying degrees beyond the control of governments, that create the context for actors' choices. These days, the balance between order and disorder is shifting toward the latter. Some of the reasons are structural, but some are the result of bad choices made by important players—and at least some of those can and should be corrected.

The chief cauldron of contemporary disorder is the Middle East. For all the comparisons that have been made to World War I or the Cold War, what is taking place in the region today most resembles the Thirty Years' War, three decades of conflict that ravaged much of Europe in the first half of the seventeenth century. As with Europe back then, in coming years, the Middle East is likely to be filled with mostly weak states unable to police large swaths of their territories, militias and terrorist groups acting with increasing sway, and both civil war and interstate strife. Sectarian and communal identities will be more powerful than national ones. Fueled by vast supplies of natural resources, powerful local actors will continue to meddle in neighboring countries' internal affairs, and major outside actors will remain unable or unwilling to stabilize the region.

There is also renewed instability on the periphery of Europe. Under President Vladimir Putin, Russia appears to have given up on the proposition of significant integration into the current European and global orders and chosen instead to fashion an alternative future based on special ties with immediate neighbors and clients. The crisis in Ukraine may be the most pronounced, but not the last, manifestation of what could well be a project of Russian or, rather, Soviet restoration.

In Asia, the problem is less current instability than the growing potential for it. There, most states are neither weak nor crumbling, but strong and getting stronger. The mix of several countries with robust identities, dynamic economies, rising military budgets, bitter historical memories, and unresolved territorial disputes yields a recipe for classic geopolitical maneuvering and possibly armed conflict. Adding to the challenges in this stretch of the world are a brittle North Korea and a turbulent Pakistan, both with nuclear

Richard N. Haass

weapons (and one with some of the world's most dangerous terrorists). Either could be the source of a local or global crisis, resulting from reckless action or state collapse.

Some contemporary challenges to order are global, a reflection of dangerous aspects of globalization that include cross-border flows of terrorists, viruses (both physical and virtual), and greenhouse gas emissions. With few institutional mechanisms available for stanching or managing them, such flows hold the potential to disrupt and degrade the quality of the system as a whole. And the rise of populism amid economic stagnation and increasing inequality makes improving global governance even more challenging.

The principles informing international order are also in contention. Some consensus exists about the unacceptability of acquiring territory by force, and it was such agreement that undergirded the broad coalition supporting the reversal of Saddam Hussein's attempt to absorb Kuwait into Iraq in 1990. But the consensus had frayed enough over the succeeding generation to allow Russia to escape similar universal condemnation after its taking of Crimea last spring, and it is anyone's guess how much of the world would respond to an attempt by China to muscle in on contested airspace, seas, or territory. International agreement on sovereignty breaks down even more when it comes to the question of the right of outsiders to intervene when a government attacks its own citizens or otherwise fails to meet its sovereign obligations. A decade after UN approval, the concept of "the responsibility to protect" no longer enjoys broad support, and there is no shared agreement on what constitutes legitimate involvement in the affairs of other countries.

To be sure, there are forces of order at work as well. There has been no great-power war for many decades, and there is no significant prospect of one in the near future. China and the United States cooperate on some occasions and compete on others, but even in the latter case, the competition is bounded. Interdependence is real, and both countries have a great deal invested (literally and figuratively) in the other, making any major and prolonged rupture in the relationship a worrisome possibility for both.

Russia, too, is constrained by interdependence, although less so than China given its energy-concentrated economy and more modest levels of external trade and investment. That means sanctions have a chance of influencing its behavior over time. Putin's foreign policy may be revanchist, but Russia's hard- and soft-power resources are both limited. Russia no longer represents anything that appeals to anyone other than ethnic Russians, and as a result, the geopolitical troubles it can cause will remain on Europe's periphery, without touching the continent's core. Indeed, the critical elements of Europe's transformation over the past 70 years—the democratization of Germany, Franco-German reconciliation, economic integration—are so robust that they can reasonably be taken for granted. Europe's parochialism and military weakness may make the region a poor partner for the United States in global affairs, but the continent itself is no longer a security problem, which is a huge advance on the past.

It would also be wrong to look at the Asia-Pacific and assume the worst. The region has been experiencing unprecedented economic growth for decades and has managed it peacefully. Here, too, economic interdependence acts as a brake on conflict. And there is still time for diplomacy and creative policymaking to create institutional shock absorbers that can help reduce the risk of confrontation stemming from surging nationalism and spiraling distrust.

The global economy, meanwhile, has stabilized in the aftermath of the financial crisis, and new regulations have been put in place to reduce the odds and scale of future crises. U.S. and European growth rates are still below historical norms, but what is holding the United States and Europe back is not the residue of the crisis so much as various policies that restrict robust growth.

North America could once again become the world's economic engine, given its stable, prosperous, and open economy; its 470 million people; and its emerging energy self-sufficiency. Latin America is, for the most part, at peace. Mexico is a far more stable and successful country than it was a decade ago, as is Colombia.

Richard N. Haass

Questions hovering over the futures of such countries as Brazil, Chile, Cuba, and Venezuela do not alter the fundamental narrative of a region heading in the right direction. And Africa, too, has a growing number of countries in which better governance and economic performance are becoming the norm rather than the exception.

Traditional analytic approaches have little to offer in making sense of these seemingly contradictory trends. One conventional route, for example, would be to frame the international dynamic as one of rising and falling powers, pitting China's advance against the United States' decline. But this exaggerates the United States' weaknesses and underestimates China's. For all its problems, the United States is well positioned to thrive in the twenty-first century, whereas China faces a multitude of challenges, including slowing growth, rampant corruption, an aging population, environmental degradation, and wary neighbors. And no other country is even close to having the necessary mix of capacity and commitment to be a challenger to the United States for global preeminence.

U.S. President Barack Obama was recently quoted as brushing off concerns that things are falling apart, noting that "the world has always been messy" and that what is going on today "is not something that is comparable to the challenges we faced during the Cold War." Such sanguinity is misplaced, however, as today's world is messier, thanks to the emergence of a greater number of meaningful actors and the lack of overlapping interests or mechanisms to constrain the capacity or moderate the behavior of the most radical ones.

Indeed, with U.S. hegemony waning but no successor waiting to pick up the baton, the likeliest future is one in which the current international system gives way to a disorderly one with a larger number of power centers acting with increasing autonomy, paying less heed to U.S. interests and preferences. This will cause new problems even as it makes existing ones more difficult to solve. In short, the post–Cold War order is unraveling, and while not perfect, it will be missed.

THE CAUSES OF THE PROBLEM

Just why have things begun to unravel? For various reasons, some structural, others volitional. In the Middle East, for example, order has been undermined by a tradition of top-heavy, often corrupt, and illegitimate governments; minimal civil society; the curse of abundant energy resources (which often retard economic and political reform); poor educational systems; and various religion-related problems, such as sectarian division, fights between moderates and radicals, and the lack of a clear and widely accepted line between religious and secular spheres. But outside actions have added to the problems, from poorly drawn national borders to recent interventions.

With more than a decade of hindsight, the decision of the United States to oust Saddam and remake Iraq looks even more mistaken than it did at the time. It is not just that the articulated reason for the war—ridding Saddam of weapons of mass destruction—was shown to be faulty. What looms even larger in retrospect is the fact that removing Saddam and empowering Iraq's Shiite majority shifted the country from balancing Iranian strategic ambitions to serving them, in the process exacerbating frictions between Sunni and Shiite Muslims within the country and the region at large.

Nor did regime change have better results in two other countries where it was achieved. In Egypt, the American call for President Hosni Mubarak to leave office contributed to the polarization of the society. Subsequent events demonstrated that Egypt was not yet ready for a democratic transition, and U.S. withdrawal of support from a longtime friend and ally raised questions elsewhere (most notably in other Arab capitals) about the dependability of Washington's commitments. In Libya, meanwhile, the removal of Muammar al-Qaddafi by a combined U.S. and European effort helped create a failed state, one increasingly dominated by militias and terrorists. The uncertain necessity of the intervention itself was compounded by the lack of effective follow-up, and the entire exercise—coming as it did a few years after Qaddafi had been

induced to give up his unconventional weapons programs—
probably increased the perceived value of nuclear weapons and reduced the likelihood of getting other states to follow Qaddafi's
example.

In Syria, the United States expressed support for the ouster of
President Bashar al-Assad and then did little to bring it about.
Obama went on to make a bad situation worse by articulating a set
of redlines involving Syrian use of chemical munitions and then
failing to act even when those lines were clearly crossed. This de-
moralized what opposition there was, forfeited a rare opportunity
to weaken the government and change the momentum of the civil
war, and helped usher in a context in which the Islamic State of
Iraq and al-Sham (ISIS), which has declared itself the Islamic
State, could flourish. The gap between rhetoric and action also further contributed to perceptions of American unreliability.

In Asia, too, the chief criticism that can be levied against U.S.
policy is one of omission. As structural trends have increased the
risks of traditional interstate conflict, Washington has failed to
move in a determined fashion to stabilize the situation—not raising the U.S. military's presence in the region significantly in order
to reassure allies and ward off challengers, doing little to build domestic support for a regional trade pact, and pursuing insufficiently
active or sustained consultations to shape the thinking and actions
of local leaders.

With regard to Russia, both internal and external factors have
contributed to the deterioration of the situation. Putin himself
chose to consolidate his political and economic power and adopt a
foreign policy that increasingly characterizes Russia as an opponent of an international order defined and led by the United States.
But U.S. and Western policy have not always encouraged more
constructive choices on his part. Disregarding Winston Churchill's
famous dictum about how to treat a beaten enemy, the West dis-
played little magnanimity in the aftermath of its victory in the
Cold War. NATO enlargement was seen by many Russians as a
humiliation, a betrayal, or both. More could have been made of the

Partnership for Peace, a program designed to foster better relations between Russia and the alliance. Alternatively, Russia could have been asked to join NATO, an outcome that would have made little military difference, as NATO has become less of an alliance in the classic sense than a standing pool of potential contributors to "coalitions of the willing." Arms control, one of the few domains in which Russia could lay claim to still being a great power, was shunted to the side as unilateralism and minimalist treaties became the norm. Russian policy might have evolved the way it has anyway, even if the United States and the West overall had been more generous and welcoming, but Western policy increased the odds of such an outcome.

As for global governance, international accords are often hard to come by for many reasons. The sheer number of states makes consensus difficult or impossible. So, too, do divergent national interests. As a result, attempts to construct new global arrangements to foster trade and frustrate climate change have foundered. Sometimes countries just disagree on what is to be done and what they are prepared to sacrifice to achieve a goal, or they are reluctant to support an initiative for fear of setting a precedent that could be used against them later. There is thus decidedly less of an "international community" than the frequent use of the phrase would suggest.

Once again, however, in recent years, developments in and actions by the United States have contributed to the problem. The post–Cold War order was premised on U.S. primacy, which was a function of not just U.S. power but also U.S. influence, reflecting a willingness on the part of others to accept the United States' lead. This influence has suffered from what is generally perceived as a series of failures or errors, including lax economic regulation that contributed to the financial crisis, overly aggressive national security policies that trampled international norms, and domestic administrative incompetence and political dysfunction.

Order has unraveled, in short, thanks to a confluence of three trends. Power in the world has diffused across a greater number and range of actors. Respect for the American economic and political model has diminished. And specific U.S. policy choices, especially in the Middle East, have raised doubts about American judgment and the reliability of the United States' threats and promises. The net result is that while the United States' absolute strength remains considerable, American influence has diminished.

WHAT IS TO BE DONE?

Left unattended, the current world turbulence is unlikely to fade away or resolve itself. Bad could become worse all too easily should the United States prove unwilling or unable to make wiser and more constructive choices. Nor is there a single solution to the problem, as the nature of the challenges varies from region to region and issue to issue. In fact, there is no solution of any sort to a situation that can at best be managed, not resolved.

But there are steps that can and should be taken. In the Middle East, the United States could do worse than to adopt the Hippocratic oath and try above all to do no further harm. The gap between U.S. ambitions and U.S. actions needs to be narrowed, and it will normally make more sense to reduce the former than increase the latter. The unfortunate reality is that democratic transformations of other societies are often beyond the means of outsiders to achieve. Not all societies are equally well positioned to become democratic at any given moment. Structural prerequisites may not be in place; an adverse political culture can pose obstacles. Truly liberal democracies may make for better international citizens, but helping countries get to that point is more difficult than often recognized—and the attempts often riskier, as immature or incomplete democracies can be hijacked by demagoguery or nationalism. Promoting order among states—shaping their foreign policies more than their internal politics—is an ambitious enough goal for U.S. policy to pursue.

But if attempts at regime change should be jettisoned, so, too, should calendar-based commitments. U.S. interests in Iraq were not well served by the inability to arrange for the ongoing presence of a residual U.S. force there, one that might have dampened the feuding of Iraqi factions and provided much-needed training for Iraqi security forces. The same holds for Afghanistan, where all U.S. forces are due to exit by the end of 2016. Such decisions should be linked to interests and conditions rather than timelines. Doing too little can be just as costly and risky as doing too much.

Other things outsiders could usefully do in the region include promoting and supporting civil society, helping refugees and displaced people, countering terrorism and militancy, and working to stem the proliferation of weapons of mass destruction (such as by trying to place a meaningful ceiling on the Iranian nuclear program). Degrading ISIS will require regular applications of U.S. airpower against targets inside both Iraq and Syria, along with coordinated efforts with countries such as Saudi Arabia and Turkey to stem the flow of recruits and dollars. There are several potential partners on the ground in Iraq, but fewer in Syria—where action against ISIS must be undertaken in the midst of a civil war. Unfortunately, the struggle against ISIS and similar groups is likely to be difficult, expensive, and long.

In Asia, the prescription is considerably simpler: implement existing policy assiduously. The Obama administration's "pivot," or "rebalance," to Asia was supposed to involve regular high-level diplomatic engagement to address and calm the region's all-too-numerous disputes; an increased U.S. air and naval presence in the region; and the building of domestic and international support for a regional trade pact. All these actions can and should be higher administration priorities, as should a special attempt to explore the conditions under which China might be prepared to reconsider its commitment to a divided Korean Peninsula.

With Russia and Ukraine, what is required is a mixture of efforts designed to shore up Ukraine economically and militarily, strengthen NATO, and sanction Russia. At the same time, Russia should also be offered a diplomatic exit, one that would include assurances that Ukraine would not become a member of NATO anytime soon or enter into exclusive ties with the EU. Reducing European energy dependence on Russia should also be a priority— something that will necessarily take a long time but should be started now. In dealing with Russia and other powers, meanwhile, Washington should generally eschew attempts at linkage, trying to condition cooperation in one area on cooperation in another. Co-operation of any sort anywhere is too difficult to achieve these days to jeopardize it by overreaching.

At the global level, the goal of U.S. policy should still be integration, trying to bring others into arrangements to manage global challenges such as climate change, terrorism, proliferation, trade, public health, and maintaining a secure and open commons. Where these arrangements can be global, so much the better, but where they cannot, they should be regional or selective, involving those actors with significant interests and capacity and that share some degree of policy consensus.

The United States also needs to put its domestic house in order, both to increase Americans' living standards and to generate the resources needed to sustain an active global role. A stagnant and unequal society will be unlikely to trust its government or favor robust efforts abroad. This need not mean gutting defense budgets, however; to the contrary, there is a strong case to be made that U.S. defense spending needs to be increased somewhat. The good news is that the United States can afford both guns and butter, so long as resources are allocated appropriately and efficiently. Another reason to get things right at home is to reduce American vulnerability. U.S. energy security has improved dramatically in recent years, thanks to the oil and gas revolutions, but the same cannot be said about other problems, such as the country's aging public infrastructure, its inadequate immigration policy, and its long-term public finances.

As has recently been noted in these pages, American political dysfunction is increasing rather than decreasing, thanks to weakened parties, powerful interest groups, political finance rules, and demographic changes. Those who suggest that the country is only a budget deal away from comity are as mistaken as those who suggest that the country is only one crisis away from restored national unity. The world can see this, and see as well that a majority of the American public has grown skeptical of global involvement, let alone leadership. Such an attitude should hardly be surprising given the persistence of economic difficulties and the poor track record of recent U.S. interventions abroad. But it is up to the president to persuade a war-weary American society that the world still matters—for better and for worse—and that an active foreign policy can and should be pursued without undermining domestic well-being.

In fact, sensible foreign and domestic policies are mutually reinforcing: a stable world is good for the home front, and a successful home front provides the resources needed for American global leadership. Selling this case will be difficult, but one way to make it easier is to advance a foreign policy that tries to reorder the world rather than remake it. But even if this is done, it will not be enough to prevent the further erosion of order, which results as much from a wider distribution of power and a decentralization of decision-making as it does from how the United States is perceived and acts. The question is not whether the world will continue to unravel but how fast and how far.

RICHARD N. HAASS is President of the Council on Foreign Relations. Follow him on Twitter @RichardHaass.

China's Imperial President

Xi Jinping Tightens His Grip

Elizabeth C. Economy

FROM OUR NOVEMBER/
DECEMBER 2014 ISSUE

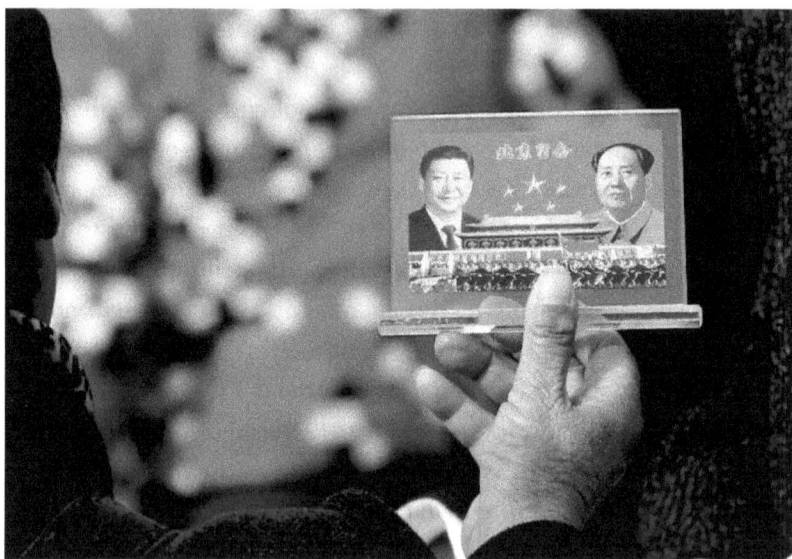

(Kimi Kyung-Hoon / Courtesy Reuters)

Chinese President Xi Jinping has articulated a simple but powerful vision: the rejuvenation of the Chinese nation. It is a patriotic call to arms, drawing inspiration from the glories of China's imperial past and the ideals of its socialist present to promote political unity at home and influence abroad. After just two years in office, Xi has advanced himself as a transformative leader, adopting an agenda that proposes to reform, if not revolutionize, political and economic relations not only within China but also with the rest of the world.

Underlying Xi's vision is a growing sense of urgency. Xi assumed power at a moment when China, despite its economic success, was politically adrift. The Chinese Communist Party, plagued by corruption and lacking a compelling ideology, had lost credibility among the public, and social unrest was on the rise. The Chinese economy, still growing at an impressive clip, had begun to show signs of strain and uncertainty. And on the international front, despite its position as a global economic power, China was punching well below its weight. Beijing had failed to respond effectively to the crises in Libya and Syria and had stood by as political change rocked two of its closest partners, Myanmar (also known as Burma) and North Korea. To many observers, it appeared as though China had no overarching foreign policy strategy.

Xi has reacted to this sense of malaise with a power grab—for himself, for the Communist Party, and for China. He has rejected the communist tradition of collective leadership, instead establishing himself as the paramount leader within a tightly centralized political system. At home, his proposed economic reforms will bolster the role of the market but nonetheless allow the state to retain significant control. Abroad, Xi has sought to elevate China by expanding trade and investment, creating new international institutions, and strengthening the military. His vision contains an implicit fear: that an open door to Western political and economic ideas will undermine the power of the Chinese state.

If successful, Xi's reforms could yield a corruption-free, politically cohesive, and economically powerful one-party state with global reach: a Singapore on steroids. But there is no guarantee that the reforms will be as transformative as Xi hopes. His policies have created deep pockets of domestic discontent and provoked an international backlash. To silence dissent, Xi has launched a political crackdown, alienating many of the talented and resourceful Chinese citizens his reforms are intended to encourage. His tentative economic steps have raised questions about the country's prospects for continued growth. And his winner-take-all mentality has undermined his efforts to become a global leader.

The United States and the rest of the world cannot afford to wait and see how his reforms play out. The United States should be ready to embrace some of Xi's initiatives as opportunities for international collaboration while treating others as worrisome trends that must be stopped before they are solidified.

A DOMESTIC CRACKDOWN

Xi's vision for a rejuvenated China rests above all on his ability to realize his particular brand of political reform: consolidating personal power by creating new institutions, silencing political opposition, and legitimizing his leadership and the Communist Party's power in the eyes of the Chinese people. Since taking office, Xi has moved quickly to amass political power and to become, within the Chinese leadership, not first among equals but simply first. He serves as head of the Communist Party and the Central Military Commission, the two traditional pillars of Chinese party leadership, as well as the head of leading groups on the economy, military reform, cybersecurity, Taiwan, and foreign affairs and a commission on national security. Unlike previous presidents, who have let their premiers act as the state's authority on the economy, Xi has assumed that role for himself. He has also taken a highly personal command of the Chinese military: this past spring, he received public proclamations of allegiance from 53 senior military officials. According to one former general, such pledges have been made only three times previously in Chinese history.

In his bid to consolidate power, Xi has also sought to eliminate alternative political voices, particularly on China's once lively Internet. The government has detained, arrested, or publicly humiliated popular bloggers such as the billionaire businessmen Pan Shiyi and Charles Xue. Such commentators, with tens of millions of followers on social media, used to routinely discuss issues ranging from environmental pollution to censorship to child trafficking. Although they have not been completely silenced, they no longer stray into sensitive political territory. Indeed, Pan, a central figure in the campaign to force the Chinese government to improve Beijing's air quality, was compelled to criticize himself on national television in 2013. Afterward, he took to Weibo, a popular Chinese microblogging service, to warn a fellow real estate billionaire against criticizing the government's program of economic reform: "Careful, or you might be arrested."

Under Xi, Beijing has also issued a raft of new Internet regulations. One law threatens punishment of up to three years in prison for posting anything that the authorities consider to be a "rumor," if the post is either read by more than 5,000 people or forwarded over 500 times. Under these stringent new laws, Chinese citizens have been arrested for posting theories about the disappearance of Malaysia Airlines Flight 370. Over one four-month period, Beijing suspended, deleted, or sanctioned more than 100,000 accounts on Weibo for violating one of the seven broadly defined "bottom lines" that represent the limits of permissible expression. These restrictions produced a 70 percent drop in posts on Weibo from March 2012 to December 2013, according to a study of 1.6 million Weibo users commissioned by The Telegraph. And when Chinese netizens found alternative ways of communicating, for example, by using the group instant-messaging platform WeChat, government censors followed them. In August 2014, Beijing issued new instant-messaging regulations that required users to register with their real names, restricted the sharing of political news, and enforced a code of conduct. Unsurprisingly, in its 2013 ranking of Internet freedom around the world, the U.S.-based nonprofit Freedom House ranked China 58 out of 60 countries—tied with Cuba. Only Iran ranked lower.

In his efforts to promote ideological unity, Xi has also labeled ideas from abroad that challenge China's political system as unpatriotic and even dangerous. Along these lines, Beijing has banned academic research and teaching on seven topics: universal values, civil society, citizens' rights, freedom of the press, mistakes made by the Communist Party, the privileges of capitalism, and the independence of the judiciary. This past summer, a party official publicly attacked the Chinese Academy of Social Sciences, a government research institution, for having been "infiltrated by foreign forces." This attack was met with mockery among prominent Chinese intellectuals outside the academy, including the economist Mao Yushi, the law professor He Weifang, and the writer Liu Yiming. Still, the accusations will likely have a chilling effect on scholarly research and international collaboration.

This crackdown might undermine the very political cohesiveness Xi seeks. Residents of Hong Kong and Macao, who have traditionally enjoyed more political freedom than those on the mainland, have watched Xi's moves with growing unease; many have called for democratic reform. In raucously democratic Taiwan, Xi's repressive tendencies are unlikely to help promote reunification with the mainland. And in the ethnically divided region of Xinjiang, Beijing's restrictive political and cultural policies have resulted in violent protests.

Even within China's political and economic upper class, many have expressed concern over Xi's political tightening and are seeking a foothold overseas. According to the China-based *Hurun Report*, 85 percent of those with assets of more than $1 million want their children to be educated abroad, and more than 65 percent of Chinese citizens with assets of $1.6 million or more have emigrated or plan to do so. The flight of China's elites has become not only a political embarrassment but also a significant setback for Beijing's efforts to lure back home top scientists and scholars who have moved abroad in past decades.

A MORAL AUTHORITY?

The centerpiece of Xi's political reforms is his effort to restore the moral authority of the Communist Party. He has argued that failing to address the party's endemic corruption could lead to the demise of not only the party but also the Chinese state. Under the close supervision of Wang Qishan, a member of the Politburo Standing Committee, tackling official corruption has become Xi's signature issue. Previous Chinese leaders have carried out anticorruption campaigns, but Xi has brought new energy and seriousness to the cause: limiting funds for official banquets, cars, and meals; pursuing well-known figures in the media, the government, the military, and the private sector; and dramatically increasing the number of corruption cases brought for official review. In 2013, the party punished more than 182,000 officials for corruption, 50,000 more than the annual average for the previous five years. Two scandals that broke this past spring indicate the scale of the campaign. In the first, federal authorities arrested a lieutenant general in the Chinese military for selling hundreds of positions in the armed forces, sometimes for extraordinary sums; the price to become a major general, for example, reached $4.8 million. In the second, Beijing began investigating more than 500 members of the regional government in Hunan Province for participating in an $18 million vote-buying ring.

Xi's anticorruption crusade represents just one part of his larger plan to reclaim the Communist Party's moral authority. He has also announced reforms that address some of Chinese society's most pressing concerns. With Xi at the helm, the Chinese leadership has launched a campaign to improve the country's air quality; reformed the one-child policy; revised the *hukou* system of residency permits, which ties a citizen's housing, health care, and education to his official residence and tends to favor urban over rural residents; and shut down the system of "reeducation through labor" camps, which allowed the government to detain people without cause. The government has also announced plans to make the legal system more transparent and to rid it of meddling by local officials.

Despite the impressive pace and scope of Xi's reform initiatives, it remains unclear whether they represent the beginning of longer-term change, or if they are merely superficial measures designed to buy the short-term goodwill of the people. Either way, some of his reforms have provoked fierce opposition. According to the *Financial Times*, former Chinese leaders Jiang Zemin and Hu Jintao have both warned Xi to rein in his anticorruption campaign, and Xi himself has conceded that his efforts have met with significant resistance. The campaign has also incurred real economic costs. According to a report by Bank of America Merrill Lynch, Chinese

GDP could fall this year by as much as 1.5 percentage points as a result of declining sales of luxury goods and services, as officials are increasingly concerned that lavish parties, political favor-buying, and expensive purchases will invite unwanted attention. (Of course, many Chinese are still buying; they are just doing so abroad.) And even those who support the goal of fighting corruption have questioned Xi's methods. Premier Li Keqiang, for example, called for greater transparency and public accountability in the government's anticorruption campaign in early 2014; his remarks, however, were quickly deleted from websites.

Xi's stance on corruption may also pose a risk to his personal and political standing: his family ranks among the wealthiest of the Chinese leadership, and according to *The New York Times*, Xi has told relatives to shed their assets, reducing his vulnerability to attack. Moreover, he has resisted calls for greater transparency, arresting activists who have pushed for officials to reveal their assets and punishing Western media outlets that have investigated Chinese leaders.

KEEPING CONTROL

As Xi strives to consolidate political control and restore the Communist Party's legitimacy, he must also find ways to stir more growth in China's economy. Broadly speaking, his objectives include transforming China from the world's manufacturing center to its innovation hub, rebalancing the Chinese economy by prioritizing consumption over investment, and expanding the space for private enterprise. Xi's plans include both institutional and policy reforms. He has slated the tax system, for example, for a significant overhaul: local revenues will come from a broad range of taxes instead of primarily from land sales, which led to corruption and social unrest. In addition, the central government, which traditionally has received roughly half the national tax revenue while paying for just one-third of the expenditures for social welfare, will increase the funding it provides for social services, relieving some of the burden on local governments. Scores of additional policy initiatives are also in trial phases, including encouraging private investment in state-owned enterprises and lowering the compensation of their executives, establishing private banks to direct capital to small and medium-sized businesses, and shortening the length of time it takes for new businesses to secure administrative approvals.

Yet as details of Xi's economic plan unfold, it has become clear that despite his emphasis on the free market, the state will retain control over much of the economy. Reforming the way in which state-owned enterprises are governed will not undermine the dominant role of the Communist Party in these companies' decision-making; Xi has kept in place significant barriers to foreign investment; and even as the government pledges a shift away from investment-led growth, its stimulus efforts continue, contributing to growing levels of local debt. Indeed, according to the Global Times, a Chinese newspaper, the increase in the value of outstanding nonperforming loans in the first six months of 2014 exceeded the value of new nonperforming loans for all of 2013.

Moreover, Xi has infused his economic agenda with the same nationalist—even xenophobic—sentiment that permeates his political agenda. His aggressive anticorruption and antimonopoly campaigns have targeted multinational corporations making products that include powdered milk, medical supplies, pharmaceuticals, and auto parts. In July 2013, in fact, China's National Development and Reform Commission brought together representatives from 30 multinational companies in an attempt to force them to admit to wrongdoing. At times, Beijing appears to be deliberately undermining foreign goods and service providers: the state-controlled media pay a great deal of attention to alleged wrongdoing at multinational companies while remaining relatively quiet about similar problems at Chinese firms.

Like his anticorruption campaign, Xi's investigation of foreign companies raises questions about the underlying intent. In a widely publicized debate broadcast by Chinese state television between the head of the European Union Chamber of Commerce in China and an official from the National Development and Reform Commission, the European official forced his Chinese counterpart to defend the seeming disparities between the Chinese government's treatment of foreign and domestic companies. Eventually, the Chinese official appeared to yield, saying that China's antimonopoly procedure was a procedure "with Chinese characteristics."

The early promise of Xi's overhaul thus remains unrealized. A 31-page scorecard of Chinese economic reform, published in June 2014 by the U.S.-China Business Council, contains dozens of unfulfilled mandates. It deems just three of Xi's policy initiatives successes: reducing the time it takes to register new businesses, allowing multinational corporations to use Chinese currency to expand their business, and reforming the *hukou* system. Tackling deeper reforms, however, may require a jolt to the system, such as the collapse of the housing market. For now, Xi may well be his own worst enemy: calls for market dominance are no match for his desire to retain economic control.

WAKING THE LION

Xi's efforts to transform politics and economics at home have been matched by equally dramatic moves to establish China as a global power. The roots of Xi's foreign policy, however, predate his presidency. The Chinese leadership began publicly discussing China's rise as a world power in the wake of the 2008 global financial crisis, when many Chinese analysts argued that the United States had begun an inevitable decline that would leave room for China at the top of the global pecking order. In a speech in Paris in March 2014, Xi recalled Napoleon's ruminations on China: "Napoleon said that China is a sleeping lion, and when she wakes, the world will shake." The Chinese lion, Xi assured his audience, "has already awakened, but this is a peaceful, pleasant, and civilized lion." Yet some of Xi's actions belie his comforting words. He has replaced the decades-old mantra of the former Chinese leader Deng Xiaoping—"Hide brightness, cherish obscurity"—with a far more expansive and muscular foreign policy.

For Xi, all roads lead to Beijing, figuratively and literally. He has revived the ancient concept of the Silk Road—which connected the Chinese empire to Central Asia, the Middle East, and even Europe—by proposing a vast network of railroads, pipelines, highways, and canals to follow the contours of the old route. The infrastructure, which Xi expects Chinese banks and companies to finance and build, would allow for more trade between China and much of the rest of the world. Beijing has also considered building a roughly 8,100-mile high-speed intercontinental railroad that would connect China to Canada, Russia, and the United States through the Bering Strait. Even the Arctic has become China's backyard: Chinese scholars describe their country as a "near-Arctic" state.

Along with new infrastructure, Xi also wants to establish new institutions to support China's position as a regional and global leader. He has helped create a new development bank, operated by the BRICS countries—Brazil, Russia, India, China, and South Africa—to challenge the primacy of the International Monetary Fund and the World Bank. And he has advanced the establishment of the Asian Infrastructure Investment Bank, which could enable China to become the leading financer of regional development. These two efforts signal Xi's desire to capitalize on frustrations with the United States' unwillingness to make international economic organizations more representative of developing countries.

Xi has also promoted new regional security initiatives. In addition to the already existing Shanghai Cooperation Organization, a Chinese-led security institution that includes Russia and four Central Asian states, Xi wants to build a new Asia-Pacific security structure that would exclude the United States. Speaking at a conference in May 2014, Xi underscored the point: "It is for the people of Asia to run the affairs of Asia, solve the problems of Asia, and uphold the security of Asia."

Xi's predilection for a muscular regional policy became evident well before his presidency. In 2010, Xi chaired the leading group responsible for the country's South China Sea policy, which broadened its definition of China's core interests to include its expansive claims to maritime territory in the South China Sea. Since then, he has used everything from the Chinese navy to fishing boats to try to secure these claims—claims disputed by other nations bordering the sea. In May 2014, conflict between China and Vietnam erupted when the China National Petroleum Corporation moved an oil rig into a disputed area in the South China Sea; tensions remained high until China withdrew the rig in mid-July. To help enforce China's claims to the East China Sea, Xi has declared an "air defense identification zone" over part of it, overlapping with those established by Japan and South Korea. He has also announced regional fishing regulations. None of China's neighbors has recognized any of these steps as legitimate. But Beijing has even redrawn the map of China embossed on Chinese passports to incorporate areas under dispute with India, as well as with countries in Southeast Asia, provoking a political firestorm.

These maneuvers have stoked nationalist sentiments at home and equally virulent nationalism abroad. New, similarly nationalist leaders in India and Japan have expressed concern over Xi's policies and taken measures to raise their countries' own security profiles. Indeed, during his campaign for the Indian prime ministership in early 2014, Narendra Modi criticized China's expansionist tendencies, and he and Japanese Prime Minister Shinzo Abe have since upgraded their countries' defense and security ties. Several new regional security efforts are under way that exclude Beijing (as well as Washington). For example, India has been training some Southeast Asian navies, including those of Myanmar and Vietnam, and many of the region's militaries—including those of Australia, India, Japan, the Philippines, Singapore, and South Korea—have planned joint defense exercises.

A VIGOROUS RESPONSE

For the United States and much of the rest of the world, the awakening of Xi's China provokes two different reactions: excitement, on the one hand, about what a stronger, less corrupt China could achieve, and significant concern, on the other hand, over the challenges an authoritarian, militaristic China might pose to the U.S.-backed liberal order.

On the plus side, Beijing's plans for a new Silk Road hinge on political stability in the Middle East; that might provide Beijing with an incentive to work with Washington to secure peace in the region. Similarly, Chinese companies' growing interest in investing abroad might give Washington greater leverage as it pushes forward a bilateral investment treaty with Beijing. The United States should also encourage China's participation in the Trans-Pacific Partnership, a major regional free-trade agreement under negotiation. Just as China's negotiations to join the World Trade Organization in the 1990s prompted Chinese economic reformers to advance change at home, negotiations to join the TPP might do the same today.

In addition, although China already has a significant stake in the international system, the United States must work to keep China in the fold. For example, the U.S. Congress should ratify proposed changes to the International Monetary Fund's internal voting system that would grant China and other developing countries a larger say in the fund's management and thereby reduce Beijing's determination to establish competing groups.

On the minus side, Xi's nationalist rhetoric and assertive military posture pose a direct challenge to U.S. interests in the region and call for a vigorous response. Washington's "rebalance," or "pivot," to Asia represents more than simply a response to China's more assertive behavior. It also reflects the United States' most closely held foreign policy values: freedom of the seas, the air, and space; free trade; the rule of law; and basic human rights. Without a strong pivot, the United States' role as a regional power will diminish, and Washington will be denied the benefits of deeper engagement with many of the world's most dynamic economies. The United States should therefore back up the pivot with a strong military presence in the Asia-Pacific to deter or counter Chinese aggression; reach consensus and then ratify the TPP; and bolster

U.S. programs that support democratic institutions and civil society in such places as Cambodia, Malaysia, Myanmar, and Vietnam, where democracy is nascent but growing.

At the same time, Washington should realize that Xi may not be successful in transforming China in precisely the ways he has articulated. He has set out his vision, but pressures from both inside and outside China will shape the country's path forward in unexpected ways. Some commodity-rich countries have balked at dealing with Chinese firms, troubled by the their weak record of social responsibility, which has forced Beijing to explore new ways of doing business. China's neighbors, alarmed by Beijing's swagger, have begun to form new security relationships. Even prominent foreign policy experts within China, such as Peking University's Wang Jisi and the retired ambassador Wu Jianmin, have expressed reservations over the tenor of Xi's foreign policy.

Finally, although little in Xi's domestic or foreign policy appears to welcome deeper engagement with the United States, Washington should resist framing its relationship with China as a competition. Treating China as a competitor or foe merely feeds Xi's anti-Western narrative, undermines those in China pushing for moderation, and does little to advance bilateral cooperation and much to diminish the stature of the United States. Instead, the White House should pay particular attention to the evolution of Xi's policies, taking advantage of those that could strengthen its relationship with China and pushing back against those that undermine U.S. interests. In the face of uncertainty over China's future, U.S. policymakers must remain flexible and fleet-footed.

ELIZABETH C. ECONOMY is C. V. Starr Senior Fellow and Director for Asia Studies at the Council on Foreign Relations.

Bitcoin Goes Boom

Will the World's Favorite Cryptocurrency Explode or Implode?

Yuri Takhteyev and
Mariana Mota Prado   JANUARY 30, 2014

An artistic representation of bitcoins. (fdecomite / Flickr)

It might not have been word of the year for 2013, but "Bitcoin" figured prominently in the shortlists. Known formerly only to true geeks, the mysterious cryptocurrency was in the news almost every day. Many of the stories were tales of riches gained and lost: a Norwegian student who discovered that the 5,600 bitcoins he purchased for $24 in 2009 were now worth $700,000; a British man who accidentally threw away a hard drive containing digital keys to bitcoins worth over $6 million. Others were tales of crime: websites where anonymous buyers could use bitcoins to buy drugs or even pool money for potential assassinations of public figures. And still others focused on attempts at regulating Bitcoin, which ranged from declaring it altogether illegal (Thailand) to embracing it wholeheartedly (Switzerland).

Why all the fuss? Much of it has to do with Bitcoin's pure novelty and its wild price fluctuations (from under $20 per bitcoin at the start of 2013 to a high of $1,203 in December to around $925 now). But above all, it is because Bitcoin is an extraordinary idea—one whose ramifications no one can fully foresee. Its foundational premise is that monetary systems do not need a central government. Instead, Bitcoin relies on clever mathematics to ensure that everyone plays by the rules. In theory, at least, no one can control Bitcoin. And this means, of course, that nobody can tell Bitcoin users what they should and shouldn't be spending their money on—for good or for ill. That presents regulating agencies with difficult questions: Should they try to control Bitcoin? Can they control it?

If all this sounds familiar, it should. The world faced these same questions in the early days of the Internet. Whether Bitcoin is more like AOL or Google, of course, is yet to be seen. Still, how governments choose to respond to it could change global finance for good.

HOW IT WORKS

Bitcoins are sometimes called virtual cash. But a better analogy is to Rai stones, a currency historically used in Yap, an island in Micronesia. Yapese used large stone disks, up to 12 feet in diameter, to pay for big transactions. Difficult to move, however, Rai stones were often just left in their place. A person using his stone to pay someone else would publicly announce the transfer of the stone's ownership. According to one anthropologist, a large stone once fell into ocean en route to the island. Rather than mourn the loss, the islanders continued to accept the stone as a valid form of payment, even though no one ever saw it again.

Bitcoin works like Rai stones hidden in the sea. The system allocates units of value, called bitcoins. Like a stone under the ocean, a bitcoin has no use other than as a form of payment. You can't touch or see it. But it has value because people agree that it does and because its numbers are limited. Around 12 million bitcoins are currently in circulation. That number can grow only by around 25,000 bitcoins per week. Such guaranteed rarity, users expect, will ensure that bitcoins retain their worth.

All forms of money require the currency to be in limited supply. Sometimes the supply is limited by nature—there is only so much gold in the world. Other times, we trust some authority to ensure it. The world relies on Washington, for example, to issue a limited supply of U.S. dollars and to punish anyone who puts out counterfeit ones. In Bitcoin's case, no centralized institutional backer is needed. It is neither a company nor an association. No one party is keeping track of account balances—the participants do it collectively, aided by clever mathematics. The scheme is based on a paper published in 2008 under the pseudonym Satoshi Nakamoto, and a piece of software released by Nakamoto in 2009. (The software is open source—anyone can inspect or modify it.) Nobody knows for sure who Nakamoto is, or even how many Nakamotos are out there. And nobody, not even Nakamoto, is fully in control. The system just proceeds by the rules defined in his paper, with rare modifications adopted by a consensus of users. The lack of centralized control makes regulating Bitcoin difficult—and intentionally so.

The 12 million bitcoins now in existence are distributed among individual accounts. Much like the Yapese and their Rai, account holders do not physically hold any bitcoins. Rather, everyone knows how many coins belong to each account, based on the public history of transfers. To transfer bitcoins, one simply announces the transfer, naming the new account. Once the announcement is confirmed, the bitcoins are understood to belong to the new account. Although all Bitcoin transactions are public, the identity of account holders is not. All anyone knows are the account numbers involved in each transaction. This creates two challenges.

The first challenge is easy to understand: How does one know that an announcement was made by the true account holder without knowing who that owner is? Bitcoin solves this first problem with so-called digital signatures, a well-worn cryptographic technique that dates to the 1970s. Each public account number comes with a secret matching key—essentially a long number that can be plugged into a mathematical formula to generate a confirmation code. The math behind this scheme allows others to verify the confirmation code without knowing the secret key. (However, if the owner of the account ever loses the secret key, as happened to the unlucky British man, then he or she can no longer transfer his or her bitcoins. In other words, the account holder still technically has the coins, but can never spend them.)

The second challenge is subtler: How do we prevent someone from gaming the system by falsifying the time stamps on his or her transfer announcements? One user could first announce a transfer of five bitcoins to a second user's account in exchange for $5,000 in cash and then announce that he or she had transferred all of his or her bitcoins to a third account the day before. The second user would be tricked into paying for bitcoins from a now empty account. The problem of verifying the true time of an announcement without the aid of a trusted overseer has stumped computer scientists for years. If some computers record that they saw an announcement yesterday and others do not, which should one trust? Nakamoto's paper finally solved the riddle with a clever combination of engineering and economics.

Bitcoin transaction announcements are recorded in so-called blocks, each block containing a record of transactions that happened in a span of roughly ten minutes. Every block ends with a mathematical puzzle. The next block must start with a solution to that puzzle to be considered valid. The resulting chain of puzzles forms an official history of all transactions.

Anyone can try to solve a puzzle. They are designed so that a computer using a simple program can figure out the answer, but only with a lot of trial and error. The difficulty of the puzzles is automatically adjusted so that, no matter how many computers are playing the game, someone hits the jackpot—successfully "mining" a block—roughly once every ten minutes. People who allow their computers to participate in this game are called miners. The lucky miner who is the first to solve the last block's problem gets a prize, currently 25 bitcoins, worth a bit over $20,000. Those 25 bitcoins are generated out of thin air, so that the total number of bitcoins grows by 25 every 10 minutes.

Whoever generates the solution is also in charge of creating the next block, which includes a record of any transfers that were announced while miners' computers were working on the last puzzle. Some of these transfer announcements will come with a small optional transaction fee—a tip from the transferor to the miner who will record the transaction. (Miners can skip transactions. The tip helps ensure diligence.) The new block defines a new puzzle to be solved by the next block. And the cycle begins again.

This scheme makes it extremely difficult to forge the history of transactions: to do so, the fraudster would need to create an alternative history of puzzle-solution pairs, one for every ten-minute period. That would require staggering computing power. Not even Google's data centers would be of much help in this task.

WHAT IS IT FOR?

There are many legitimate uses for Bitcoin. It offers a simple and secure payment method: the payer is fully in control of how much money is transferred and when, so there is no reason to worry about unauthorized charges or identity theft. In the last year, many companies—including Overstock.com, Newegg, and, most recently, TigerDirect—announced that they would start accepting bitcoins as payment. Wider adoption of Bitcoin could help put a dent in a fraud problem that costs merchants billions of dollars every year.

Bitcoin's transparent and decentralized design also helps new players to enter the highly centralized and byzantine world of electronic payments and allows them to do things that would have been difficult otherwise. For example, a number of firms are starting to use Bitcoin for remittance payments, bypassing traditional gatekeepers and offering their services at a fraction of the rates charged by companies such as Western Union. (The global remittances to developing countries add up to hundreds of billions of dollars.)

Yet not all of Bitcoin's implications are positive. Its promise of anonymity also makes the currency very attractive for illegal transactions.

One famous example of this is Silk Road, an online marketplace for illegal drugs and stolen credit cards that has been in operation since 2011. Briefly shut down by U.S. law enforcement in 2013 (only to be relaunched a month later), Silk Road attracted media attention for openly flouting the law. Processing a little over a million dollars' worth of illegal transactions every month, however, Silk Road represents a relatively meager sort of criminality. Bitcoin might also become a tool for large-scale money laundering. In other words, it could be used for transactions that are not illegal per se but that help disguise the origins of funds obtained through illegal activities. If Bitcoin can, in fact, deliver what it promises, international efforts to stamp out large-scale crime and corruption might take a serious hit.

Consider a typical large corruption scheme: A company wants to bribe an elected official with $10 million, in order to "win" a contract worth 50 times as much. Both parties want to make the deal, but how would they actually make the payment? It is hard to physically transfer $10 million in cash inconspicuously (over 200 pounds of paper in hundred-dollar bills). Wiring that much money is also risky. In recent years, many jurisdictions have started to require financial institutions to monitor their clients' activities and alert authorities about anything considered suspicious. Such regulation often requires especially close monitoring of high-risk individuals such as current and former elected officials. People who engage in money laundering usually know that all of their transactions may be closely watched.

The most practical solution today involves sending the money through corporate vehicles, trusts, or nonprofit entities. The company offering the bribe sets up an offshore shell company, which then makes a wire transfer to a trust fund that names a person connected to the official (a family member or a friend) as a beneficiary. Such schemes can, indeed, tie up investigators but even they have become increasingly risky with the expansion of international anti-money-laundering and anticorruption regulation.

Bitcoin promises a seemingly unbeatable solution: if the corrupt company can obtain $10 million worth of bitcoins, it can transfer those from their own anonymous account to one controlled by the corrupt official. Nobody would know where the money went. Not even the company that paid the bribe would be able to prove that the account into which it transfered bitcoins belongs to the official. And as long as the official was careful, the bribe could never be seized by the government or stolen.

In practice, of course, using bitcoins for such large bribes is not easy. One problem is the relatively small volume of dollar-to-bitcoin trade, which means that anyone attempting to make a large payment may have trouble doing so without adversely affecting the exchange rate. The fact that Bitcoin transactions are public also means that sophisticated analysis can undermine anonymity of users who do not take careful steps to cover their tracks. Nor can Bitcoin protect users from many traditional police tools, such as informants or sting operations. Finally, the volatility of the dollar-to-bitcoin exchange rate remains a major problem: within the last three months, the value of one bitcoin has oscillated between $200 and $1,200. (Those fluctuations, of course, also make it harder to use Bitcoin for many legitimate activities.) Such problems, however, may turn out to be much simpler than those presented by alternative money-laundering methods. And they could further dissipate with growing use of Bitcoin. As more people use the currency, the price will likely be more stable and exchanging large amounts would present less of a challenge.

IS IT GOOD?

With all Bitcoin's potential for good and ill, it might well make sense to try to regulate it. But would that be possible? Bitcoin's decentralized structure makes oversight difficult. The government cannot order Bitcoin to flag suspicious transactions, since it is not a legal entity but a network of participants, many of whom are anonymous. Of course, the same used to be said of the Internet, yet today, almost every country on the planet enforces rules for online conduct. And although people can sometimes get away with breaking the law online, the get caught quite often. Similarly, there are several ways for governments to cope with Bitcoin. These steps will not prevent every instance of wrongdoing, but they will make each more challenging.

The crudest approach would be to simply prohibit the use of Bitcoin and similar systems. (For example, the central banks of Iceland and Thailand have declared the use of Bitcoin software to be illegal in those countries, although neither country appears to be set on enforcing the ban.) Treating Bitcoin software as a criminal tool and punishing people for using or having it would deter many users. Sure, you might never get caught, but most people wouldn't want the risk. The downside, of course, is that this would also eliminate any potential benefits of the legal uses of Bitcoin as well, such as security and low fees. After all, paper money is also a key tool of money laundering, yet governments do not ban it, recognizing the many conveniences that it offers.

A milder version of such prohibition would be to allow personal use but ban financial institutions from engaging in Bitcoin transactions, as China did in December 2013. This would not affect the use of Bitcoin for smaller crime but would put a dent in large-scale schemes. Again, however, it would also eliminate many of the currency's benefits. It is also worth remembering that no regulator can fully control today's global finance sector. If the United States bans American banks from trading bitcoins, Swiss banks would be happy to take the extra customers. And if the United States manages to strong-arm Switzerland into the same regulatory regime, other countries will be standing in line.

Another solution would be to closely monitor Bitcoin transactions. Financial institutions could be asked to record all transactions involving Bitcoin and to report anything suspicious. Since the chain of Bitcoin transfers within the network is public, policing the endpoints of the system (where bitcoins are converted into traditional money, goods, or services) might make it possible to link any official offering a bribe to the one receiving it. For instance, the U.S. government announced in March 2013 that any financial institution issuing or exchanging virtual currencies would be subject to the same monitoring and reporting rules as regular financial institutions. And it has recently showed that it is serious about enforcing compliance. Such regulations may be quite effective in discouraging money laundering. Unfortunately, they may also endanger some legitimate uses: smaller companies might lack resources to implement the mandated tracking, leaving the market to the larger institutions that are less interested in pursuing innovative solutions based on Bitcoin.

A subtler approach would be for the government to work with large Bitcoin players. Although Bitcoin was meant to be fully decentralized, in practice, most transactions today pass through a handful of accounts. Shutting them down might be ineffective, since new ones would take their place. Working with them, however, could be productive. Eager to maintain their current position, the large players may agree to self-regulate rather than decide to take a stand and risk a more heavy-handed response from the authorities. Such self-regulation could involve modifying the Bitcoin protocol to reduce anonymity.

WHAT IT MEANS

Whatever the fate of Bitcoin, it is worth remembering that it is only the first (and the most well-known) of several distributed cryptocurrencies in existence today. Such alternatives range from the likes of Dogecoin, a cryptocurrency whose most notable difference from Bitcoin is the use of a whimsical dog logo, to Zerocoin, which promises a substantially higher degree of anonymity. Without a doubt, there will be many more in the coming months and years.

Different cryptocurrencies will likely find different uses. Those that allow for a large degree of oversight (perhaps through some form of self-regulation) might enter the mainstream. Others that make oversight exceptionally hard might be ideal for truly illegal activities but find themselves shut out of the mainstream as a result. And a range of cryptocurrencies operating between these extremes could come on the market.

Today, no one knows what Bitcoin and other cryptocurrencies will bring. The situation harks back to the early days of the Internet, when expectations for the new technology ranged from utter skepticism to wild pipe dreams. Cryptocurrencies are likely here to stay, although they might look very different two decades from now. Bitcoin could turn out to be the cryptocurrency equivalent of CompuServe or AOL—revolutionary for its time, only to be forgotten later when a better technology emerged. Or it could turn out to be like Amazon.com, making the best of its first-mover's advantage and dominating the industry for years. Cryptocurrencies will probably not bring about the libertarian rapture promised by some proponents—but ignore them at your own peril.

YURI TAKHTEYEV is an assistant professor (status only) at the University of Toronto's Faculty of Information and Chief Software Architect at Rangle.io. He is the author of Coding Places: Software Practice in a South American City.

MARIANA MOTA PRADO is an associate professor at the Faculty of Law, University of Toronto, and the co-author (with Michael Trebilcock) of What Makes Poor Countries Poor? Institutional Determinants of Development.

Erdogan Loses It

How the Islamists Forfeited Turkey

Halil Karaveli   FEBRUARY 9, 2014

Erdogan walks in front of a military honor guard, February 8, 2011.
(Courtesy Reuters)

The Turkish state changed hands a decade ago, when Islamic conservatives (supported by the liberals) prevailed in elections against
the country's old guard, the rightist nationalists known as Kemal-
ists. It may be about to do so again. The conservative alliance of
Prime Minister Recep Tayyip Erdogan's Justice and Development
Party (AKP) and the movement of Fethullah Gülen, a Muslim
cleric who leads his congregation from self-imposed exile in the
United States, has imploded. As it does, the military is gearing up
to insert itself into politics once more.

The trouble started in 2011, when Erdogan decided to purge most Gülen supporters from the AKP party list ahead of the general election in June. No longer willing to share power with anyone else, Erdogan also ousted most liberals and supporters of the moderate President Abdullah Gül. Then, a subsequent reform of the public administration served as an excuse to remove many Gülenists from key bureaucratic posts.

The Gülenists' response came in February 2012, when a prosecutor believed to be affiliated with the movement tried to summon Hakan Fidan, the head of the National Intelligence Organization and a close confidant of Erdogan, for questioning over his role in then-secret negotiations between the Turkish government and the Kurdistan Workers' Party (PKK). The Gülenists had made their opposition to talks with the Kurdish movement known and wanted to derail them by charging Erdogan's envoy—and by implication the prime minister himself—with treason.

Last summer, the rift between the two groups widened as protesters occupied Gezi Park. Gülen-affiliated media criticized Erdogan, comparing him to a "pharaoh." The government, with its reputation tarnished and Gülenists gaining the upper hand, announced in late 2013 that it would shut down Gülen-operated schools. That would have deprived the movement of its main source of revenue and recruits. Not ready to take the hit lying down, the Gülen movement retaliated by supporting a corruption probe, led by the prosecutor Celal Kara, against relatives of several cabinet ministers and businessmen with close ties to the government. Upping the ante, Erdogan launched a full-scale purge of any suspected Gülen sympathizers from sensitive positions in the bureaucracy, judiciary, and police.

Coalitions may come and go, but authoritarianism is forever—or so it seems in Turkey.

Gülen, of course, insists that he does not wield any power over state officials and claims that his only concern is for the public. Yet in an exceptionally fiery sermon last December, Gülen excoriated those "who turn a blind eye to the thief while punishing those who prosecute the thieves," beseeching God to "consume their homes with fire, destroy their nests, break their accords." Even Gülenists do not deny the existence of an informal network of devotees within the state. That was the bargain between the AKP and the Gülenists all along: In return for its support—votes and the endorsement of the AKP by Gülenist media—the Gülen movement would get to staff the state bureaucracy. In fact, the AKP needed the Gülenists' well-educated cadres to run Turkey, especially its police and judiciary. And since 2008, Gülenist sympathizers in the police and among prosecutors have helped put hundreds of regime opponents in prison.

Now, with the AKP-Gülenist relationship broken, Erdogan accuses his former allies of having established a parallel state that defies the authority of the elected government and of staging a coup against him. His most recent move against the so-called parallel state was his attempt last month to enact a law that would subordinate the judiciary to the executive, disabling his enemies from launching further probes. That will suit the Erdogan family just fine: A prosecutor tried to detain Erdogan's son at the end of last year. The police, instructed by the government, refused to carry out the order, and the prosecutor was subsequently reassigned. More than 2,000 police officers and nearly 100 prosecutors have been reassigned since last December.

The conflict between Erdogan and the Gülen movement might sound quite byzantine. But remember that this is the land that gave us the term. Indeed, the dispute follows a historical pattern. The Ottoman Sultans feared autonomous powers such as religious congregations. Mehmet II, the conqueror of Constantinople, was particularly repressive; he curtailed economic freedoms in a bid to disempower religious fraternities. Kemal Atatürk, the founder of the republic, was obsessed with pacifying religious congregations, wanting to ensure that they could never rival the state. Turkish Foreign Minister Ahmet Davutoglu even defended the ongoing purges by pointing to history. Turkish state tradition, he said, includes the practice of "sacrificing sons for the state," to eliminate potential rivals for the throne.

Now, leading commentators in the AKP's media inform that the ruling party hopes to forge new alliances—particularly with the military, its old enemy. But Erdogan should remember that turning to the military to help quash opposition is not risk-free. In 1971, conservative Prime Minister Süleyman Demirel solicited help from the military to quash the left, only to end up out of power. Erdogan has instructed the Ministry of Justice to prepare for a retrial of imprisoned military officers. The generals may very well be acquitted.

It is easy to see how this will play out. After several years of silence, the Turkish General Staff has once again taken to issuing political statements. The military high command has called the judiciary to task after Erdogan's chief adviser confessed that several military officers had been convicted on trumped-up charges. It has demanded a retrial of the officers and issued sharp condemnations of critics. Many observers fear that the state's institutional breakdown will invite the generals to intervene and "restore order," as they have done so many times before. Stoking those fears: In a letter to a newspaper editor last month, Necdet Özel, the chief of the General Staff, wrote that ensuring the functioning of the parliamentary system has been "the basic principle" of the armed forces, stressing that the military is determined to uphold it because "we want peace in our country." The statement begged the question of what the military will do if there is no peace in the country. Military interventions in the past have always been motivated by an alleged determination to ensure the preservation of democracy.

The return of the old military is not the only risk. There is also a new military to take into account. Since Islamic conservatives won control of the state apparatus and subdued the military in 2007 and 2008, purges from within the military of suspected Islamists—which used to take place once a year—have ceased. It may be inferred from this that there are now likely many within the military who sympathize with Gülen. His message, which combines Islam and Turkish patriotism particularly appeals to officers, who generally hail from conservative family backgrounds. And mass imprisonments of top generals, which have depleted the military's upper ranks, have made it possible for younger officers to rise further and faster than ever. The Gülenist clout within the military might be considerable. Erdogan would hope that the top brass, to whom he now appeals, will succeed in keeping Gülenists among the lower ranks in check. But he must also fear a move against him by younger officers acting outside the chain of command. That was what happened in 1960, when the authoritarian Prime Minister Adnan Menderes was toppled.

Beyond that, the AKP-Gülenist backbiting represents a massive and collective failure of the Islamic conservative movement, from which none of its components may be able to recover. The corruption charges have deprived the AKP of any remaining moral authority. And the turf war has shattered the government's reputation for managerial competence. The Gülenists have lost moral capital, too. The movement has always taken pains to show itself as standing above petty politics. But revelations of the extent of its power within the state undermine that point. The Gülenists have shaken Erdogan, but they may have also undone themselves. Their maneuvering does not inspire confidence in all of Turkey: According to a recent poll, only six percent of the public supports the Gülenists' case against the AKP, whereas 28.5 percent supports the ruling party, and 45 percent thinks that both the AKP and the Gülenists are at fault.

Coalitions may come and go, but authoritarianism is forever—or so it seems in Turkey. The Turkish Islamists' failure as managers of the state will most likely catapult the traditional custodians of the state, the rightist nationalists in the military and the bureaucracy who enjoy a considerable following in society, back to power.

HALIL KARAVELI is a Senior Fellow at the Central Asia-Caucasus Institute and the Silk Road Studies Program, which are affiliated with the School of Advanced International Studies at Johns Hopkins University and the Institute for Security and Development Policy. He is also Managing Editor of the Turkey Analyst.

Putin's Brain

Alexander Dugin and the Philosophy Behind Putin's Invasion of Crimea

Anton Barbashin
and Hannah Thoburn   MARCH 31, 2014

Russian President Vladimir Putin in 2007. (Damir Sagolj / Courtesy Reuters)

Since the collapse of the Soviet Union, Russia has searched fruitlessly for a new grand strategy—something to define who Russians are and where they are going. "In Russian history during the 20th century, there have been various periods—monarchism, totalitarianism, perestroika, and finally, a democratic path of development," Russian President Boris Yeltsin said a couple of years after the collapse of the Soviet Union, "Each stage has its own ideology," he continued, but now "we have none."

To fill that hole, in 1996 Yeltsin designated a team of scholars to work together to find what Russians call the *Russkaya ideya*

("Russian idea"), but they came up empty-handed. Around the same time, various other groups also took up the task, including a collection of conservative Russian politicians and thinkers who called themselves *Soglasiye vo imya Rossiya* ("Accord in the Name of Russia"). Along with many other Russian intellectuals of the day, they were deeply disturbed by the weakness of the Russian state, something that they believed needed to be fixed for Russia to return to its rightful glory. And for them, that entailed return to the Russian tradition of a powerful central government. How that could be accomplished was a question for another day.

Russian President Vladimir Putin, to whom many of the *Soglasiye* still have ties, happened to agree with their ideals and overall goals. He came to power in 1999 with a nationwide mandate to stabilize the Russian economy and political system. Thanks to rising world energy prices, he quickly achieved that goal. By the late 2000s, he had breathing room to return to the question of the Russian idea. Russia, he began to argue, was a unique civilization of its own. It could not be made to fit comfortably into European or Asian boxes and had to live by its own uniquely Russian rules and morals. And so, with the help of the Russian Orthodox Church, Putin began a battle against the liberal (Western) traits that some segments of Russian society had started to adopt. Moves of his that earned condemnation in the West—such as the criminalization of "homosexual propaganda" and the sentencing of members of Pussy Riot, a feminist punk-rock collective, to two years in prison for hooliganism—were popular in Russia.

True to Putin's insistence that Russia cannot be judged in Western terms, Putin's new conservatism does not fit U.S. and European definitions. In fact, the main trait they share is opposition to liberalism. Whereas conservatives in those parts of the world are fearful of big government and put the individual first, Russian conservatives advocate for state power and see individuals as serving that state. They draw on a long tradition of Russian imperial conservatism and, in particular, Eurasianism. That strain is authoritarian in essence, traditional, anti-American, and anti-European; it values religion and public submission. And more significant to to-day's headlines, it is expansionist.

After the collapse of the Soviet Union, ultranationalist ideologies were decidedly out of vogue.

RUSSIAN ROOTS

The roots of Eurasianism lie in Russia's Bolshevik Revolution, although many of the ideas that it contains have much longer histories in Russia. After the 1917 October Revolution and the civil war that followed, two million anti-Bolshevik Russians fled the country. From Sofia to Berlin and then Paris, some of these exiled Russian intellectuals worked to create an alternative to the Bolshevik project. One of those alternatives eventually became the Eurasianist ideology. Proponents of this idea posited that Russia's Westernizers and Bolsheviks were both wrong: Westernizers for believing that Russia was a (lagging) part of European civilization and calling for democratic development; Bolsheviks for presuming that the whole country needed restructuring through class confrontation and a global revolution of the working class. Rather, Eurasianists stressed, Russia was a unique civilization with its own path and historical mission: To create a different center of power and culture that would be neither European nor Asian but have traits of both. Eurasianists believed in the eventual downfall of the West and that it was Russia's time to be the world's prime exemplar.

In 1921, the exiled thinkers Georges Florovsky, Nikolai Trubetzkoy, Petr Savitskii, and Petr Suvchinsky published a collection of articles titled Exodus to the East, which marked the official birth of the Eurasianist ideology. The book was centered on the idea that Russia's geography is its fate and that there is nothing any ruler can do to unbind himself from the necessities of securing his lands. Given Russia's vastness, they believed, its leaders must think imperially, consuming and assimilating dangerous populations on every border. Meanwhile, they regarded any form of democracy, open economy, local governance, or secular freedom as highly dangerous and unacceptable.

In that sense, Eurasianists considered Peter the Great—who tried to Europeanize Russia in the eighteenth century—an enemy and a traitor. Instead, they looked with favor on Tatar-Mongol rule, between the thirteenth and fifteenth centuries, when Genghis Khan's empire had taught Russians crucial lessons about building a strong, centralized state and pyramid-like system of submission and control.

Eurasianist beliefs gained a strong following within the politically active part of the emigrant community, or White Russians, who were eager to promote any alternative to Bolshevism. However, the philosophy was utterly ignored, and even suppressed in the Soviet Union, and it practically died with its creators. That is, until the 1990s, when the Soviet Union collapsed and Russia's ideological slate was wiped clean.

THE EVOLUTION OF A REVOLUTIONARY

After the collapse of the Soviet Union, ultranationalist ideologies were decidedly out of vogue. Rather, most Russians looked forward to Russia's democratization and reintegration with the world.

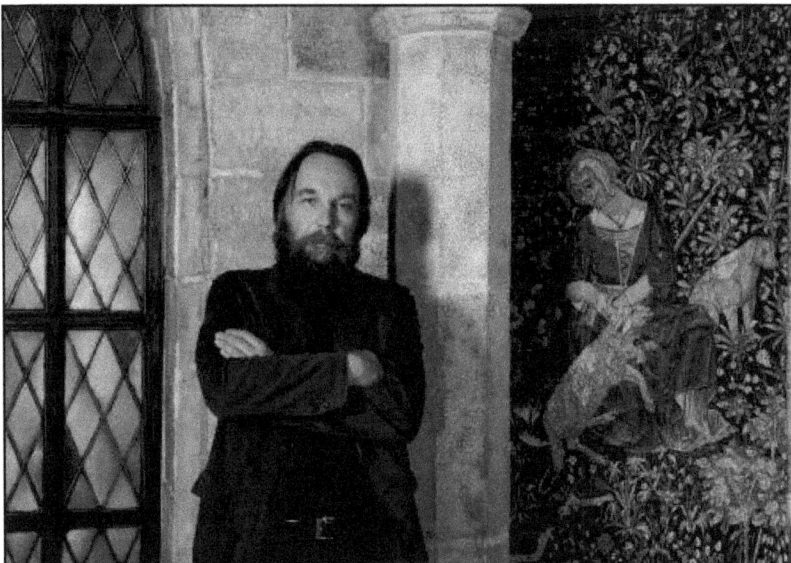

Alexander Dugin. (Dugin.ru)

Still, a few hard-core patriotic elements remained that opposed de-Sovietization and believed—as Putin does today—that the collapse of the Soviet Union was the greatest geopolitical catastrophe of the century. Among them was the ideologist Alexander Dugin, who was a regular contributor to the ultranationalist analytic center and newspaper *Den'* (later known as *Zavtra*). His earliest claim to fame was a 1991 pamphlet, "The War of the Continents," in which he described an ongoing geopolitical struggle between the two types of global powers: land powers, or "Eternal Rome," which are based on the principles of statehood, communality, idealism, and the superiority of the common good, and civilizations of the sea, or "Eternal Carthage," which are based on individualism, trade, and materialism. In Dugin's understanding, "Eternal Carthage," was historically embodied by Athenian democracy and the Dutch and British Empires. Now, it is represented by the United States. "Eternal Rome" is embodied by Russia. For Dugin, the conflict between the two will last until one is destroyed completely—no type of political regime and no amount of trade can stop that. In order for the "good" (Russia) to eventually defeat the "bad" (United States), he wrote, a conservative revolution must take place.

His ideas of conservative revolution are adapted from German interwar thinkers who promoted the destruction of the individualistic liberal order and the commercial culture of industrial and urban civilization in favor of a new order based on conservative values such as the submission of individual needs and desires to the needs of the many, a state-organized economy, and traditional values for society based on a quasi-religious view of the world. For Dugin, the prime example of a conservative revolution was the radical, Nazi-sponsored north Italian Social Republic of Salò (1943–45). Indeed, Dugin continuously returned to what he saw as the virtues of Nazi practices and voiced appreciation for the SS and Herman Wirth's occult Ahnenerbe group. In particular, Dugin praised the orthodox conservative-revolutionary projects that the SS and Ahnenerbe developed for postwar Europe, in which they envisioned a new, unified Europe regulated by a feudal system of ethnically separated regions that would serve as vassals to the German suzerain. It is worth noting that, among other projects, the Ahnenerbe was responsible for all the experiments on humans in the Auschwitz and Dachau concentration camps.

Between 1993 and 1998, Dugin joined the Russian nationalist legend Eduard Limonov in creating the now banned National-Bolshevik Movement (later the National-Bolshevik Party, or NBP), where he became the chief ideologist of a strange synthesis of socialism and ultra-right ideology. By the late 1990s, he was recognized as the intellectual leader of Russia's entire ultra-right movement. He had his own publishing house, Arktogeya ("Northern Country"), several slick Web sites, a series of newspapers and magazines, and published The Foundation of Geopolitics, an immediate best seller that was particularly popular with the military.

Since the early 2000s, Dugin's ideas have only gained in popularity. Their rise mirrors Putin's own transition from apparent democrat to authoritarian.

Dugin's introduction to the political mainstream came in 1999, when he became an adviser to the Russian parliamentarian Gennadii Seleznev, one of Russia's most conservative politicians, a two-time chairman of the Russian parliament, a member of the Communist Party, and a founder of the Party of Russia's Rebirth. That same year, with the help of Vladimir Zhirinovsky, leader of Russia's nationalist and very misnamed Liberal Democratic Party of Russia, Dugin became the chairman of the geopolitical section of the Duma's Advisory Council on National Security.

But his inclusion in politics did not necessarily translate to wider appeal among the politics of the elite. For that, Dugin had to transform his ideology into something else—something uniquely Russian. Namely, he dropped the most outrageous, esoteric, and radical elements of his ideology, including his mysticism, and drew instead on the classical Eurasianism of Trubetzkoy and Savitskii. He set to work creating the International Eurasian Movement, a group that would come to involve academics, politicians, parliamentarians, journalists, and intellectuals from Russia, its neighbors, and the West.

TO EUROPE AND BEYOND

Like the classical Eurasianists of the 1920s and 1930s, Dugin's ideology is anti-Western, anti-liberal, totalitarian, ideocratic, and socially traditional. Its nationalism is not Slavic-oriented (although Russians have a special mission to unite and lead) but also applies to the other nations of Eurasia. And it labels rationalism as Western and thus promotes a mystical, spiritual, emotional, and messianic worldview.

But Dugin's neo-Eurasianism differs significantly from previous Eurasianist thought. First, Dugin conceives of Eurasia as being much larger than his predecessors ever did. For example, whereas Savitskii believed that the Russian-Eurasian state should stretch from the Great Wall of China in the east to the Carpathian Mountains to the west, Dugin believes that the Eurasian state must incorporate all of the former Soviet states, members of the socialist block, and perhaps even establish a protectorate over all EU members. In the east, Dugin proposes to go as far as incorporating Manchuria, Xinxiang, Tibet, and Mongolia. He even proposes eventually turning southwest toward the Indian Ocean.

In order to include Europe in Eurasia, Dugin had to rework the enemy. In classical Eurasianist thought, the enemy was the Romano-Germanic Europe. In Dugin's version, the enemy is the United States. As he writes: "The USA is a chimerical, anti-organic, transplanted culture which does not have sacral state traditions and cultural soil, but, nevertheless, tries to force upon the other continents its anti-ethnic, anti-traditional [and] "babylonic" model." Classical Eurasianists, by contrast, favored the United States and even considered it to be a model, especially praising its economic nationalism, the Monroe Doctrine, and its non-membership in the League of Nations.

Another crucial point of difference is his attitude toward fascism and Nazi Germany. Even before World War II, classical

Eurasianists opposed fascism and stood against racial anti-Semitism. Dugin has lauded the state of Israel for hewing to the principles of conservativism but has also spoken of a connection between Zionism and Nazism and implied that Jews only deserved their statehood because of the Holocaust. He also divides Jews into "bad" and "good." The good are orthodox and live in Israel; the bad live outside of Israel and try to assimilate. Of course, these days, those are views to which he rarely alludes in public.

PUTIN'S PLAY

Since the early 2000s, Dugin's ideas have only gained in popularity. Their rise mirrors Putin's own transition from apparent democrat to authoritarian. In fact, Putin's conservative turn has given Dugin a perfect chance to "help out" the Russian leader with proper historical, geopolitical, and cultural explanations for his policies. Recognizing how attractive Dugin's ideas are to some Russians, Putin has seized on some of them to further his own goals.

Although Dugin has criticized Putin from time to time for his economic liberalism and cooperation with the West, he has generally been the president's steadfast ally. In 2002, he created the Eurasia Party, which was welcomed by many in Putin's administration. The Kremlin has long tolerated, and even encouraged, the creation of such smaller allied political parties, which give Russian voters the sense that they actually do live in a democracy. Dugin's party, for example, provides an outlet for those with chauvinistic and nationalist leanings, even as the party remains controlled by the Kremlin. At the same time, Dugin built strong ties with Sergei Glazyev, who is a co-leader of the patriotic political bloc Rodina and currently Putin's adviser on Eurasian integration. In 2003, Dugin tried to become a parliamentary deputy along with the Rodina bloc but failed.

Although his electoral foray was a bust, some voters' positive reception to his anti-Western projects encouraged Dugin to forge ahead with the Eurasianist movement. After the shock of Ukraine's Orange Revolution in 2004, he created the Eurasianist Youth

Union, which promotes patriotic and anti-Western education. It has 47 coordination offices throughout Russia and nine in countries in the Commonwealth of Independent States, Poland, and Turkey. Its reach far exceeds that of any existing democratic-oriented movement.

In 2008, Dugin was made a professor at Russia's top university, Moscow State University, and the head of the national sociological organization Center for Conservative Studies. He also appears regularly on all of Russia's leading TV channels, commenting on both domestic and foreign issues. His profile has only increased since the pro-democracy protests of the winter of 2011–12 and Putin's move around the same time to build a Eurasian Union. His outsized presence in Russian public life is a sign of Putin's approval; Russian media, particularly television, is controlled almost entirely by the Kremlin. If the Kremlin disapproves of (or not longer has a use for) a particular personality, it will remove him or her from the airwaves.

Dugin and other like-minded thinkers have wholeheartedly endorsed the Russian government's action in Ukraine, calling on him to go further and take the east and south of Ukraine, which, he writes, "welcomes Russia, waits for it, pleads for Russia to come." The Russian people agree. Putin's approval ratings have climbed over the past month, and 65 percent of Russians believe that Crimea and eastern regions of Ukraine are "essentially Russian territory" and that "Russia is right to use military force for the defense of the population." Dugin, then, has proven to be a great asset to Putin. He has popularized the president's position on such issues as limits on personal freedom, a traditional understanding of family, intolerance of homosexuality, and the centrality of Orthodox Christianity to Russia's rebirth as a great power. But his greatest creation is neo-Eurasianism.

Dugin's ideology has influenced a whole generation of conservative and radical activists and politicians, who, if given the chance, would fight to adapt its core principles as state policy. Considering the shabby state of Russian democracy, and the country's continued move away from Western ideas and ideals, one might argue that the chances of seeing neo-Eurasianism conquer new ground are increasing. Although Dugin's form of it is highly theoretical and deeply mystical, it is proving to be a strong contender for the role of Russia's chief ideology. Whether Putin can control it as he has controlled so many others is a question that may determine his longevity.

ANTON BARBASHIN is a Moscow-based international relations researcher and analyst.

HANNAH THOBURN is a Eurasia analyst at the Foreign Policy Initiative.

Foreign Policy à la Modi

India's Next Worldview

Manjari Chatterjee Miller   APRIL 3, 2014

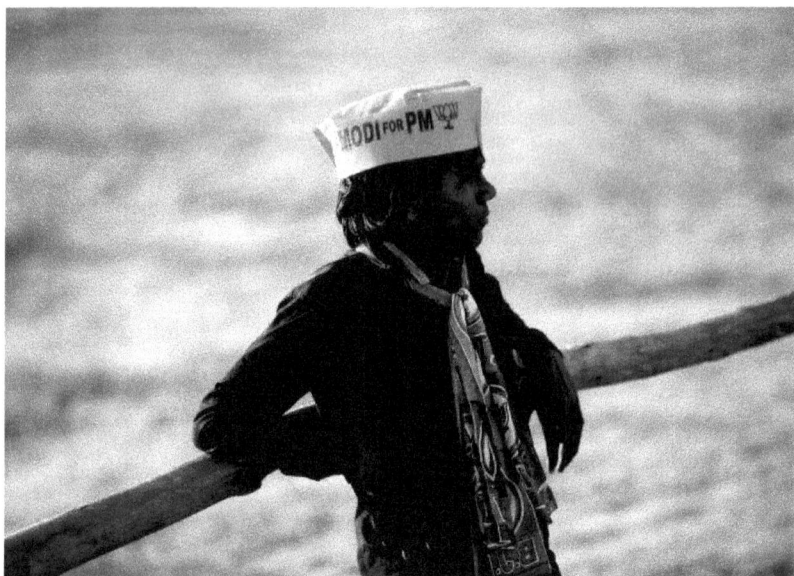

A Modi supporter after a rally in Gurgaon on the outskirts of New Delhi, April 3, 2014. (Adnan Abidi / Courtesy Reuters)

Between April 7 and May 12, some 814 million Indian voters will have a chance to exercise their fundamental democratic rights by selecting a new government. In a country that has faced scrutiny for its chaotic administration, contentious politics, and vast inequity, the democratic process will unfold in routine and expected ways. Despite India's massive corruption problems, the ballot will be mostly free and fair. Voter turnout from all classes, and particularly the poor, will be substantial. Following a more recent precedent, no single party will gain an absolute majority in parliament. And, in the aftermath of a relatively smooth transfer of power, the new government will take the reins and begin the task of forming a cabinet.

Predictability also applies to foreign policy. Observers in the United States blanch at the prospect of a Prime Minister Narendra Modi, the candidate of the right-wing Bharatiya Janata Party (BJP), whom they believe may apply his Hindutva, or Hindu nationalist, beliefs to Indian foreign policy. Their worry is shared by many Indians, who believe him to be at best indifferent to, and at worst hostile to, the concerns of Indian Muslims. What the effect of a Modi government would be on Indian domestic politics is an open question. But no matter who assumes the country's highest office, the broad contours of Indian foreign policy are not likely to change dramatically.

ALL THE SAME

A look at Indian foreign policy since 1964 confirms that it has been characterized more by continuity than by change. And even those changes that have occurred, while important, have been incremental, and unrelated to the political ideology of the party in power. After all, as a serving Indian ambassador recently told me, "An elephant is not prone to making sharp turns."

India's top defense relationship continues to be with Russia. No matter what Russia does in its own region, it seems, India will not rock the boat.

For many years, much to the Indian government's annoyance, the country's relationship with Pakistan defined India on the world stage. Despite regime changes in New Delhi and Islamabad and numerous diplomatic initiatives, cease-fires, and bilateral talks, Kashmir's status is as unresolved today as it was 50 years ago, and relations continue to be overtly hostile, with the ever-present possibility of war. Although the conflict is often framed as one between Hindus and Muslims, a secular Congress Party–led government has been no more or less likely to be conciliatory toward Pakistan than a Hindu Nationalist BJP-led government. In fact, three major peace initiatives with Pakistan occurred under

BJP prime minister Atal Bihari Vajpayee's watch: "bus diplomacy" in 1999, the Agra summit in 2001, and the Islamabad summit in 2004.

China is another neighbor that is a thorn in India's side. Prior to 1960, India and China were good friends. Popular slogans such as *"Hindi-Chini bhai-bhai"* (Indians and Chinese are brothers) encapsulated their joint opposition to imperialism and colonial powers; Indian socialist leaders admired Mao; and India even allegedly refused a permanent seat in the United Nations Security Council as a show of solidarity with communist China, whose UN seat had been given to the Republic of China (Taiwan). But the 1962 war between the two over their shared Himalayan border irrevocably damaged Sino-Indian relations and led to a border conflict that is still unresolved today. India continues to see China as the major threat, a view that is shared across party lines. In 1998, when the BJP government tested nuclear weapons, Prime Minister Vajpayee wrote a letter to President Clinton citing China as the main motivation. And, despite the economic gains in the relationship since, incidents such as China's incursions over the border in April 2013, weeks before Chinese Prime Minister Li Keqiang was due to visit India, have not helped the government trust its northern neighbor more. As a powerful former Indian foreign secretary remarked to me recently, "Pakistan is just an enemy. China is the adversary."

As for the United States, New Delhi's relations with Washington are marked by ongoing mutual suspicion, but, despite that, there is little chance of armed conflict between them. There have certainly been pragmatic shifts in the relationship: the rapid increase in bilateral trade, from $6 billion in 1990 to $86 billion in 2011; the 2005 signing of the Indo-U.S. nuclear deal that allowed for civil nuclear cooperation; and the United States' designation of India as a rising power and a strategic partner. However, India's steadfast reluctance to actually be that strong ally whose military closely cooperates with the United States has baffled Washington for years. And U.S. President Barack Obama's relatively cool shoulder to India during the Congress years has not helped.

Like India's major bilateral relations, its ties to other countries have remained steady over the years, no matter the party in power. India's top defense relationship continues to be with Russia. No matter what Russia does in its own region, it seems, India will not rock the boat. Shiv Shankar Menon, India's national security adviser, recently said of Ukraine, "We hope that whatever internal issues there are within Ukraine are settled peacefully . . . there are legitimate Russian and other interests involved." India's refusal to support "unilateral measures" against the Russian government prompted Russian President Vladimir Putin to specifically thank India for its support.

India's relations with Israel and Iran have likewise stayed stable. After India established formal diplomatic relations with Israel in 1992, a shift initiated by the Congress Party and endorsed and deepened by the subsequent BJP government, Israel rapidly became its second-largest defense supplier. But India continues to vote, as it always has, against Israel in the United Nations General Assembly. No Indian head of state, no matter the party, has yet set foot in Tel Aviv. In 2005, meanwhile, India finally bowed to U.S. pressure and voted at the IAEA to refer Iran to the UN Security Council, a move it repeated in 2006 and 2009. Yet Iran and India have historically had a conflict-free relationship, and that continues to this day. In 2013, two Iranian warships and a submarine paid a goodwill visit to Mumbai.

In other words, the broad shape of Indian foreign policy has remained the same for nearly five decades. And the shifts that do occur are not sudden and have rarely, if ever, been political. The Indian nuclear tests in 1998 under a BJP government, for example, are often cited as a dramatic reversal on the country's previous nuclear stance, and are attributed primarily to the Hindutva ideology of the BJP government. However, as a 2004 paper by K. Subramanyam, former director of the Institute for Defense Studies and Analysis, pointed out, India's nuclear arsenal was made operational by Congress leader Narasimha Rao's government. It was only divisions among the scientific community that led to a lack of consensus on whether to test and prevented Rao from doing so. And the tests themselves unified Indian parties across the political spectrum in jubilation.

Similarly, there is a perception among observers, as a Western intelligence official with experience of India said to me, that Congress Prime Minister Manmohan Singh was courageous to "burn political capital" and respond to President George W. Bush's initiation of a shift in the relationship with India. Between 2005 and 2008, Bush implemented the civil nuclear cooperation agreement with India, recognized India's security concerns, and emphasized its importance as a rising power. In return, Singh decided to change the tone of a bilateral relationship that had never been smooth. Still, Bush's overtures to India started before Singh came to power. A former Indian ambassador to a Western country confirmed to me that Brajesh Mishra, who had been national security adviser to the outgoing BJP government, and Jaswant Singh, who had variously held the positions of minister of finance, minister of external affairs, and minister of defense, had been highly receptive to Bush's initial outreach.

When Bush stepped down, Indian journalist Ashok Malik emphasized the former president's popularity across the Indian political spectrum, calling him "the best American president India has ever had." Since then, the relationship has grown somewhat frostier—not because Indian politics have changed (they haven't) but because American politics have. Both major Indian parties believe that the Obama administration has done little to soothe tensions between the countries, and are unified on issues such as the Devyani Khobragade case, in which an Indian diplomat in New York was accused of exploiting her children's nanny and arrested and strip-searched by U.S. authorities.

STATE OF PLAY

All this is not to say that Indian foreign policy is unchangeable. Irrespective of which party forms the government, state politics, administrative capacity, and the individuals who are appointed by the prime minister to key offices will matter a great deal for foreign policy.

Both major Indian parties believe that the Obama administration has done little to soothe tensions between the countries.

India is a federal system with 28 states and seven union territories. Most foreign observers understand how that affects domestic policy, but not why it matters for foreign policy. And regional issues can be a major driver in India's foreign policy. India's relations with Bangladesh, for example, can hinge on how the chief minister of the Indian state of West Bengal responds to a boundary settlement or a water sharing agreement with Bangladesh. In 2011, Mamata Banerjee, chief minister of West Bengal, opposed the Teesta River water sharing treaty, an agreement between India and Bangladesh. Her intransigence—she was breaking with the federal government's policy on the agreement—nearly derailed Singh's first-ever visit to Bangladesh. And that was despite the fact that her party, the Trinamool Congress, was a part of the United Progressive Alliance, the coalition that presently forms the Congress Party–led central government.

Tensions between India and Sri Lanka have increased, thanks to local state politics. Indian fishermen in the Palk Straits between southern India and Sri Lanka are regularly apprehended by the Sri Lankan navy, which claims that they are in Sri Lanka's territorial waters. The Indian government alleges that the Sri Lankan navy is responsible for the deaths of some fishermen, the jailing of others, and, in some cases, fishermen's mysterious disappearances. The fishermen are Tamil, and because of that, the two major state parties in the state of Tamil Nadu, despite being bitter foes, have come together to pressure the New Delhi to take a hard line on Sri Lanka. For issues such as these, the hue of the political party or coalition in power at the center is irrelevant.

Pressure from state governments aside, the winning party or coalition will have another important problem to deal with. India's foreign policy establishment is severely understaffed. Indian Foreign Service (IFS) officials admit they are constantly firefighting—that is, responding to immediate issues rather than strategizing about the future. Foreign diplomats have noticed the problem and claim that it hurts India's performance in negotiations and meetings. Individual Indian diplomats can be excellent, a senior diplomat from a Western country who was, until recently, stationed in New Delhi told me, "However, the lack of people has led to serious hampering of policy and forces many diplomats to cling on to old ways of thinking and doing things because they don't have enough time and energy to change outmoded patterns. In India, diplomats will hang up on you mid-conversation, not return phone calls, not reply to emails." He continued that, in negotiations, India "will turn up with two people," whereas "China is better equipped. Many more people will turn up for meetings. They will be a well-drilled, well-organized group. In turn, India has a reputation of being difficult [which has] become a substitute for time and resources."

The former foreign secretary with whom I spoke agrees that the IFS needs more people. Some change is already underway: in August 2008, the government created 314 new posts. At the same time, the cabinet approved a 43 percent increase in the sanctioned batch of IFS recruits. However, any plans for expansion need to include an overhaul in training, as well as the creation of a new research and policy division. Quick expansion has led to the hiring of less able recruits without, for example, English-language skills.

Simultaneously, the lack of emphasis on strategic vision, which is one of the consequences of understaffing, can be addressed with the creation of a research wing. India's Ministry of External Affairs used to have a much-consulted "historical division," as officers refer to it, which focused on strategy. For example, it prepared India's case in the last border negotiations with China, in 1960. But the body has since disappeared. "It became extinct like the cheetah," the former foreign secretary told me with a rueful laugh. Whether these much needed administrative changes will be made by the new prime minister remains to be seen. Incoming political leaders, as the former foreign secretary said, are "not usually aware of this need for reform, and focus on the more prominent issues, such as corruption." What will really matter if Modi comes to power is the team he puts in place, particularly the national security adviser and the minister of external affairs.

Not all ministers are created equal. Both Indian IFS officers and foreign officials stated to me that a recent minister of external affairs appointed by Singh was "inexperienced" at best and "incompetent" at worst. The opposite could be said of the former and current finance ministers Pranab Mukherjee ("hard to understand sometimes, but extremely shrewd," according to the senior diplomat) and P. Chidambaram ("very capable"). That also goes for national security adviser Shiv Shankar Menon ("he is key in the India-China relationship, is an experienced China hand, and knows people like Dai Bingguo and Yang Jiechi," the Western senior intelligence official told me). Similarly, under the last BJP government, national security adviser Brajesh Mishra "multiplied Vajpayee's effectiveness several times over," according to a former Indian ambassador.

If the Congress stays in power, which, according to a recent Pew Center survey, seems unlikely given the 3:1 preference for the BJP over the ruling party, some of these issues may be addressed. For example, the government already initiated the expansion of the IFS, demonstrating that the government is aware of the problem. However, the Congress coalition government has been in power for almost a decade, and the pace of reform has not been promising.

In the event of a BJP government, the assessment of both foreign and Indian officials is that Modi is a very astute leader. In conversations, they seem very hopeful at the prospect of him becoming prime minister. "He is very dynamic," the senior diplomat to India said of Modi. "What worked in Gujarat will translate to the national scene. He will take risks." The former foreign secretary concurs. "He understands globalization, will not be blindsided, and he will be influenced by the overseas Gujarati diaspora, who are very active and networked." And, this official added, Modi "respects the bureaucracy," which bodes well for a politician with little foreign policy experience. How much he allows himself to be guided by top bureaucrats and whom he appoints will be important. Although his preferences for specific posts are mostly unknown, it was suggested to me that his national security adviser would likely be a retired bureaucrat, either from the Ministry of External Affairs or the national security apparatus. One rumored candidate, Ajit Doval, is a decorated officer and was the director of the Intelligence Bureau (India's internal intelligence agency) from 2004 to 2005. Doval currently heads the Vivekananda International Foundation, a New Delhi–based think tank.

In these conversations, some officials, both Indian and foreign, did express discomfort with what they believed to be Modi's complicity in the 2002 Gujarat massacre. But they also believed that the Singh government had lost its way. Certainly, the shadow of the Gujarat riots makes Modi a very different political figure from the last BJP prime minister, Vajpayee. However, if Modi were to assume office, any hint of less than complete acceptance of his status as prime minister by the United States would be seen as an unforgivable insult, not just by the Indian elites who support him but by those who do not. And Washington should remember that, at least in the past five decades, Indian foreign policy has been broadly consistent and any changes had little to do with the prime minister's political ideology.

MANJARI CHATTERJEE MILLER is Assistant Professor of International Relations at Boston University. She is the author of Wronged by Empire: Post-imperial Ideology and Foreign Policy in India and China.

The Price of Poverty

Psychology and the Cycle of Need

Johannes Haushofer JULY 15, 2014

Refugees who fled the conflict in Sudan's Darfur region to eastern Chad gather water at a well as a dust storm approaches, June 2008. (Finbarr O'Reilly / Courtesy Reuters)

Poverty is powerful. For those within its grasp, it alters every aspect of existence. People who happen to be born poor consume less than those born rich. They have worse access to education and healthcare and frequent exposure to corruption, extortion, and violence. An average person born in a place like Sub-Saharan Africa lives in a very different world than an average American.

But does poverty affect the way people feel, think, and act? This seems like an obvious question, and indeed, it is neither new nor mine: over the centuries, scientists, policymakers, and writers have asked whether poverty has psychological and behavioral consequences. Yet for many years, the question has been difficult to study because asking it has often been confused with blaming the poor for their poverty or attributing to them deficiencies that caused it. One prominent example is a 1965 report by Daniel Patrick Moynihan, who was assistant secretary of labor at the time, entitled "The Negro Family: The Case for National Action." In the paper, Moynihan argued that many poor black families in the United States were caught in a "tangle of pathology"—a combination of absent parents, low educational attainment, unemployment, and delinquency—and urged Washington to step in. Although Moynihan's aim was to describe external circumstances that made it difficult to escape poverty, not inherent deficiencies within poor families themselves, he was widely perceived as blaming the victims. As a result, his analysis was broadly panned.

In recent years, scholars and the public have become more willing to examine the nuances of the link between poverty and mental well-being. One reason for that is a change in the focus of such studies. Whereas Moynihan wrote about race, today's scholars write about poverty, which is less socially charged. Meanwhile, the emergence of behavioral economics has made it possible to systematically examine the ways in which decision-making can—and does—depart from the standard neoclassical model of economic behavior. Such research has made academics and policymakers more open to the idea that behavior can be affected by outside factors, poverty among them. Finally, large survey efforts such as the World Values Survey and the Gallup World Poll and sophisticated randomized field experiments spearheaded by institutions such as MIT's Jameel Poverty Action Lab have made it possible to approach social questions with more data and unprecedented rigor. As a result, asking about the psychological and behavioral consequences of poverty is no longer confused with blaming the victims, but is instead seen as the first step in solving the problem.

What, then, have we learned with this newfound freedom to explore the connection? First, that poverty does, indeed, have psychological consequences. In particular, it leads to stress and negative emotions such as sadness and anger. Those are, of course, bad outcomes in their own right. But they are also linked to economic problems. Stress is intimately connected to depression, which has severe costs for labor productivity. The best current estimates suggest that depression—through absenteeism and lost productivity—costs Europe and the United States up to one percent of GDP every year. Second, it turns out that stress and negative emotions also decrease people's willingness to make long-term investments, for instance in health and education. Together, these dynamics may create a psychological poverty trap that can keep people mired in destitution.

MONEY DOES BUY HAPPINESS

When I tell people that I study the effect of poverty on psychological well-being, I am often confronted with the notion of the "happy poor." Some people, even today, could describe "Africans" as "always smiling" and therefore happy, with a superficiality usually reserved for discussing dolphins. In this view, the poor live simple but fulfilled lives in a village where a small plot of land gives enough food to survive, a horde of children provide old-age pension, and a rich social network protects against economic shocks. As the seventeenth-century poet John Dryden put it, the poor are seen as the "guiltless men, that danced away their time/ Fresh as their groves and happy as their climes."

Until recently, the best available scientific evidence suggested that such views might be correct. In 1974, the renowned economist Richard Easterlin published a paper titled "Does Economic Growth Improve the Human Lot?" in which he summarized survey data on the relationship between income and happiness from 19 countries. The data, he wrote, show that there is, indeed, a positive relationship between income and happiness within countries, but not across them; in other words, rich people in a given society appeared happier than poor people in the same society, but richer countries did not appear happier, on average, than poorer countries. This early finding provided fodder to the romantic view that money does not buy happiness.

However, the small datasets available at the time led early researchers to the wrong conclusion. In a series of recent studies, the economists Daniel Sacks, Betsey Stevenson, and Justin Wolfers revisited the relationship between income and psychology. They analyzed responses from more than 139,000 people in 131 countries, and their findings are crystal clear: there is a positive relationship between income and emotional well-being both within and across societies. In other words, the romantic notion of the happy poor is simply not borne out by the data. Rich countries are happier than poor countries, and rich people in a given country are happier than poor people in the same country.

Of course, these studies don't have anything to say about causation—that is, whether poverty makes people unhappy or whether unhappiness makes them unproductive and, consequently, poor. (Plus there may be a third factor, such as religious beliefs, that affects both income and psychological well-being.) The only way to establish causality is to find either a natural experiment, in which one of the variables changes for random reasons, or a true experiment, in which researchers manipulate one of the variables experimentally.

A good natural experiment to test whether changes in wealth lead to changes in psychological well-being is the lottery. Are lottery winners, who are by definition randomly chosen, happier after they get their cash than non-winners? There is no shortage of folklore claiming that they are not: stories of winners losing their friends to greed, their spouses to alcohol and gambling, and their money to spending sprees and bad planning. They end up lonely and bankrupt.

There are certainly a number of high-profile individual cases and early research to support this story. A 1978 study showed that lottery winners were no happier than non-winners; in fact, non-winners found more pleasure in everyday things than winners. However, the study included only 22 lottery winners and 22 non-winners, with response rates of only 52 percent and 41 percent, respectively, which makes the results impossible to interpret.

More recent research paints an entirely different picture: Jonathan Gardner and Andrew Oswald, economists at the University of Warwick, studied the effect of winning the lottery on a group of more than 33,000 British lottery players. Those who won more than 1,000 pounds (roughly $1,700) did significantly better on the General Health Questionnaire, a measure of psychological well-being.

One problem with this study is that psychological well-being is self-reported, which can lead to bias. For instance, people might be motivated to tell researchers what they think the interviewers want to hear. In this way, lottery winners might feel a duty to report that they are happy; after all, who are they to shrug off a large windfall? Recently, a Swedish team of researchers got around this problem in an ingenious study that capitalized on the Swedish bureaucracy's obsession with data collection: in Sweden, the government knows not only who won the lottery (and how much) but also who consumed which mental health drugs. The economists David Cesarini, Robert Östling, Björn Wallace, and Erik Lindqvist used this information to show that lottery winners consumed fewer mental health drugs, especially anxiety medications, following their wins. More evidence that lotteries do not spell doom comes from another study of lottery winners in Florida, which showed that the bankruptcy rates of winners are no different from those of non-winners.

Of course, lottery players are hardly representative of all of the world's poor. But governments and charities around the world are busy conducting another natural experiment through unconditional cash transfers—an increasingly popular method of delivering assistance to the poor in which cash is sent directly to households without any strings attached. The logic behind these transfers, set out in a recent *Foreign Affairs* article by Christopher Blattman and Paul Niehaus, is that households know best what they need to buy, and giving them cash (rather than livestock or food) allows them to buy it. A typical cash-transfer program distributes funds to all households in a village that meet specified eligibility criteria—such as a grass roof, a common proxy for poverty. Because very few refuse the money, recipients are a representative sample of this segment of the population.

To understand the effects of such transfers on psychological well-being, Jeremy Shapiro, now a researcher at Princeton, and I conducted a field experiment that observed two groups of poor households in Kenya in 2012–3. One group, which included 500 households, received transfers averaging $720 each from the charity GiveDirectly, roughly equal to five months' worth of their income. The other group, containing 1,000 households, received nothing. When asked a year later, members of the first group reported a significant upswing in happiness and life satisfaction as well as a reduction in stress and depression relative to members of the second group. To deal with biases related to self-reported data, we also measured participants' levels of cortisol, the stress hormone, before and after the transfers. We found that certain types of transfers—especially larger amounts and transfers to women—reduced cortisol levels.

CHOOSING WISELY

The fact that poverty can cause stress is bad enough in its own right. But compounding the problem, stress can also be harmful economically. For one, because it is closely linked to depression, it can lead to poor work performance. Also, on a more subtle level, poverty can hinder decision-making in two key ways.

First, as the economist Sendhil Mullainathan and the psychologist Eldar Shafir explain in their recent book, living in poverty engenders a mindset of scarcity: it pushes people to focus on salient, pressing issues at the expense of others that may be just as important but not equally urgent. For instance, Indian farmers who are worried about a drought and a failing harvest might not prioritize vaccinating their children, which might be just as pivotal for their economic well-being in the long run.

Compounding this problem, destitution comes with more responsibilities than affluent people may realize. As the development economist Esther Duflo has pointed out, in rural Kenya water does not come out of the ground already sanitized, unlike the water that comes out of taps in the West. Farmers in Kenya have to go out of their way to make the water drinkable—and may easily forget to do so in the presence of more acute concerns. Critical tasks are neglected, not because the poor consider them unimportant, but because they simply don't have the bandwidth to attend to every one. According to Shafir and Mullainathan, this effect is so strong that it impairs cognitive performance in general. Together with the economist Anandi Mani and the psychologist Jiaying Zhao, they found that Indian sugarcane farmers experienced a dip in IQ just around the time when they were the poorest—namely just before the harvest.

The second way in which poverty may have an impact on economic outcomes is through its influence on stress and negative affect (an umbrella term used by psychologists to describe negative emotions such as sadness and anger). For instance, the Harvard psychologist Jennifer Lerner showed in a series of landmark studies that such negative emotions can cause people to prefer short-term rewards over long-term ones. In a typical experiment, participants were invited into a testing room, where they were shown a video clip that induced sadness. They were then asked whether they preferred to receive a smaller amount of money in the near future or a larger amount later in time. Those who had watched a sadness-inducing video were less willing to delay gratification than others who had watched a neutral video. Conversely, feelings of gratitude, induced by asking participants to recount their positive past experiences, made people more willing to tolerate delays.

A similar rise in impatience appeared when a team of researchers (including me) experimentally raised levels of the stress hormone cortisol in participants by administering its precursor hydrocortisone. Other researchers have found that people are not only more impatient but also more risk-averse when they experience stress or after hydrocortisone administration. The same goes for exposure to stressful events in the real world. As studies by researchers from the University of California at San Diego and South Korea's Sogang University recently showed, wartime trauma leads to risk-averse behavior.

BREAKING THE VICIOUS CYCLE

The psychological feedback loop that keeps the poor trapped in poverty thus has three links: poverty causes stress and negative emotions, which lead to shortsighted and risk-averse decision-making, which can, in turn, exacerbate poverty. The findings are still preliminary, and other factors—such as adverse climates, corruption, and weak rule of law—certainly play a role in perpetuating the condition. But it is not too early to draw a few lessons from the new research for policymakers trying to break the vicious cycle.

The first is that variables such as stress and happiness are important metrics of success for development programs. New indicators, both self-reported and biometric, offer hope of tracking the welfare of poor people more directly than the established metrics (such as income and consumption) and should be used in concert with them. Thus, if a program does not affect economic outcomes but offers psychological benefits (such as an intervention to combat domestic violence), it may well be worth considering. Conversely, a program that delivers economic advantages but hampers psychological well-being may have reduced value as a policy tool. For instance, although microloans can help a family start a business, the pressure to repay them generates stress—a factor that donors should consider when assessing their value.

Second, policymakers should ask whether improvements in psychological well-being can raise economic welfare, and by how much. Only a handful of trials have examined the efficacy of mental health interventions in developing countries, and the information they provide about the effects of improving mental health on economic outcomes is incomplete. Conducting further research on this topic is all the more important given the strong link between poverty and mental health.

Collecting such evidence would allow better comparison of potential donor initiatives. For instance, we might find that giving cash to the poor is more effective in alleviating their stress and depression than trying to target stress and depression directly. Or we might find that the opposite is true. Either conclusion would allow donors and policymakers to better focus their efforts. Once that happens, the same amount of development aid will benefit more people, and we will take another small step toward making poverty less powerful.

JOHANNES HAUSHOFER is an assistant professor of psychology and public affairs at Princeton University.

Meet Pakistan's Lady Cadets

The Trials and Triumphs of Women in Pakistan's Military Academy

Aeyliya Husain   AUGUST 17, 2014

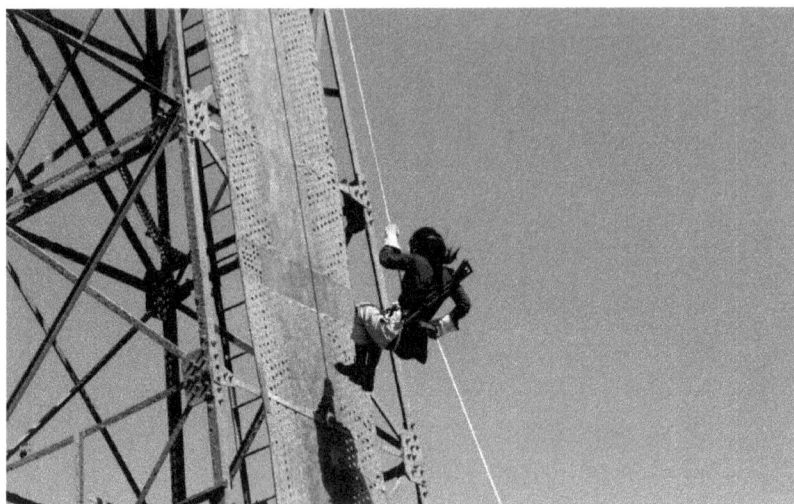

A female police cadet in Karachi, December 16, 2013. (Athar Hussain / Courtesy Reuters)

Wardah Nur never imagined that she would become a soldier. And, until ten years ago, she couldn't have.

Yet here she was, in the cool air of the Himalayan foothills, among sergeants shouting orders and cadets falling quickly into formation. They pivot, turn, and march. Only four weeks into training, though, they struggle to stay in step.

Nur belongs to a small, elite group—the 2013 "lady cadets," as they are called—the latest batch of women to train at the Pakistan Military Academy since it began accepting them in 2006 during General Pervez Musharraf's presidency. Hundreds of women vie for a spot each year, although only 32 seats are open to them. There are 2,000 seats at the academy for men. And, although men can enroll after high school, women must first earn a bachelor's degree and speak fluent English. The differences don't end there: Once enrolled, male cadets spend two years training for the battlefield, whereas female recruits train for just six months and are forbidden from direct combat. Instead, they graduate mostly to army support jobs in engineering, IT, or communications.

Nur, a slim and serious 24-year-old with a degree in electrical engineering from Pakistan's National University of Sciences and Technology, traveled nearly 300 miles to train here in Kakul, some 4,000 feet above the valley. "This opportunity was not handed to me," she says. "I had to compete for it."

Nur came to the academy by way of Mandi Bahauddin, a small and old-fashioned town in the central province of Punjab, where horse-driven carts still outnumber cars, and where girls have no place to continue their education past high school. When Nur was 16 years old, her father moved the family to Rawalpindi, a larger

Wardah Nur trains at the Pakistan Military Academy, June 2013. (Courtesy Aeyliya Husain)

city near Islamabad, where she could stay in school. Her plight was not unusual: Of all countries in the world, Pakistan has the second-largest number of children without access to schools—5.4 million—which includes 75 percent of primary-school-age girls. Most women have trouble finding jobs, and many are pushed into becoming teachers or housewives.

By joining the military, Nur and the other female cadets have guaranteed themselves employment for at least the next seven years, the required term of service.

Yet this is a bittersweet victory, as being a woman comes with difficulties outside of school and within it. Case in point: Bilal, a male cadet who will graduate with Nur and who did not give his last name, said he would never marry a female soldier. "I would prefer if she were interested in something else," he said. "Someone has to look after the children."

But Nur doesn't mind such comments. Already past the national average age of marriage, she has no interest in becoming a house-wife. She prefers the discipline of the army, and, she'll admit with a smile, she's partial to the uniform.

SAFETY FIRST

Since the first class of women cadets enrolled in 2006, roughly 330 have graduated from the academy. But this is nothing compared to the thousands of male graduates. It can be uncomfortable being in the minority, Nur says, especially when men pervade the campus. "There's always a level of insecurity," she says.

Often, though, there is little time to think about comfort. The cadets must concern themselves, first and foremost, with national security. Pakistan was the target of more terrorist attacks in 2012 than any other country in the world, and the mountains surrounding the school are constantly monitored for terrorist activity. The academy sits in the heart of a conflict zone, just north of Abbottabad, where U.S. Navy SEALs killed Osama bin Laden in 2011.

In the past 67 years, since Pakistan's partition from India in 1947, its military has grown into the country's most powerful institution, and it receives generous grants of up to $2 billion from the United States each year. Today it is the seventh-largest military in the world.

Here, at the gateway to the Silk Road, the academy produces some of the nation's best officers, many of whom have been hesitant to allow women into the club. When Musharraf opened the academy to women eight years ago, officers such as Lieutenant Colonel Usman Kayani were skeptical. "Our military was all male, and military training has always been for men," he said. Yet few wanted to question Musharraf, then the country's top-ranking general, and so women began to train, performing, for the most part, the same tasks as the men.

Four months into training, Nur's batch of cadets has moved on to field exercises. Out in the plains of the Punjab, they dig trenches, plan defensive maneuvers, and keep an eye out for insurgents. Here, under the blazing September sun, where temperatures reach 100 degrees Fahrenheit by mid-afternoon, months of learning in the classroom are put to the test. Playing war games with tanks, fighter jets, and artillery fire, the women are the closest they will ever come to the battlefield.

In the field, it is Nur's job to lead reconnaissance missions—her award for excelling in the classroom. It is a delicate task, as many cadets resent that she has earned so much responsibility. But Nur knows when to be strict and when to ignore their pointed glares; above all, she won't let anything get in the way of her graduating with distinction. So, she guides her classmates as they live in the trenches, forsaking sleep to analyze maps and devise battle plans.

One night, she leads a group of five cadets on a mission to assess the best plan for the next day's attack. They navigate the fields in complete darkness, with only Nur's map and binoculars as guides. Under her leadership, the team spots potential enemy posts and creates a feasible plan of attack.

"Wardah has the qualities to be a good leader," says platoon commander Arooj Arif, who graduated from the military academy two years ago and now trains the new recruits. "She was very good from the start."

After five days in the field, the cadets are back at the academy, readying themselves for graduation. Alongside her classmates, Nur receives her post-graduation assignment: She will work as an army engineer in Rawalpindi, a densely populated city in Punjab, where she will analyze thermal images from the battlefield. Unless the law changes, she's done with combat.

THIS IS THE MOMENT

The day before graduation, October 11, 2013, is a tense one. In the dormitories, the women cadets pack their suitcases and exchange email addresses. Tomorrow, their parents, aunts, uncles, and cousins will join Pakistan's visiting dignitaries and top military brass on the academy lawn. And Nur will find out whether the army chief will award her the Commandant's Cane, the honor reserved for the year's top female cadet. Three other prizes will be awarded, but this is the only one that will go to a woman.

"I won't be able to sleep tonight," Nur says, laying out her uniform. "When I was young, I would get up early to watch the ceremony on television. I never thought I'd one day be a part of it."

Sleep or no, tomorrow arrives. The cadets run through the halls, their uniforms clean and crisp, their long hair pulled back into buns beneath their berets. They help each other with last-minute fixes: adjusting hair ties, straightening collars, tightening belts. All the while a crowd pours into the stands surrounding the drill square. This is it, the day the women have been working toward and the parade that many consider the most impressive in the country.

The women, dressed and ready, form a line outside their dormitories, where a staff sergeant waits to inspect them. Once cleared, the women march toward the drill square, comprising a small raft in a sea of male cadets. "When we march in, the first thing on our minds is, 'this is the moment,'" Nur says. "Everybody's excited, everybody's anxious.

In the square, Nur takes her place as the sword bearer and awaits the announcement. Her commander speaks: "There are so many ladies who excel in academics, who excel in military exercises, who excel in physical tests," he says. "But there is only one who is all-rounded, who is at the top." He calls Nur's name, and, standing up a little straighter, she marches up to receive the honor.

Later, the celebration is like any other. The cadets cry, hug their friends, and find their parents, beaming, on the lawn. Nur's mother wipes tears from her eyes. Her father brims with pride. "It's not so easy to win that award," he says. "It means she was born a soldier."

Back in her dorm, Nur changes out of her uniform into civilian attire: a bright tunic and flowing trousers. She replaces her beret with a hijab. Then, she picks up her duffle bag and looks around the room one last time before closing the door.

AEYLIYA HUSAIN is a documentary filmmaker based in Toronto.

Notes From the Underground

The Long History of Tunnel Warfare

Arthur Herman AUGUST 26, 2014

A Palestinian fighter from the Izz el-Deen al-Qassam Brigades, the armed wing of the Hamas movement, is seen inside an underground tunnel in Gaza on August 18, 2014. (Courtesy Reuters)

Perhaps the most surprising development of the recent war between Israel and Gaza was the discovery of the sophisticated network of tunnels that Hamas had quietly developed in the preceding years. The dark, low-tech tunnels running underneath Gaza offered a stark juxtaposition to the modern artillery Israel deployed on the surface.

But if the tunnels hinted at an older kind of warfare, that doesn't mean they should be dismissed as a military curiosity. Compared with the most sophisticated weapons systems in use today, tunnels have withstood the test of time: for centuries, they have allowed military units to approach their enemies undetected and helped weaker combatants turn the battlefield to their advantage. There's no way to know how long drones or lasers or anti-missile defense systems will last. But as long as there is warfare, tunnels will almost certainly be part of the fight.

FROM ANTIQUITY TO MODERNITY

Tunnels and caves, tunnels' geologic predecessor, have a long history in warfare stretching back to biblical times. For at least 3,000 years, embattled populations have used them to hide from, and strike at, stronger enemies. Ironically, this has been especially so in the region where present-day Israel and Palestine are located. Archaeologists have found more than 450 ancient cave systems in the Holy Land, including many that were dug into mountainsides, which the Jews used to launch guerrilla-style attacks on Roman legionnaires during the Great Jewish Revolt from AD 66 to 70. The Romans faced the same tactic around that time in their fight along the Rhine and Danube frontiers in Europe, against Germanic tribes who would dig hidden trenches connected by tunnels and then spring out of the ground to ambush the Roman soldiers.

But the use of tunnels hasn't been limited to insurgencies. It wasn't long before the Roman Empire began using them as an offensive weapon in siege warfare. By digging a hidden trench right up to a city's walls, and then tunneling underneath to undermine the walls and force a breach, the Romans discovered that it was possible to end a siege long before the city's population was starved into submission by blockade.

Unsurprisingly, perhaps, the use of tunnels in this manner soon inspired the development of countertunnels. The ancient Roman historian Polybius described a siege in 189 BC at the Greek city of Ambracia, where the Romans began digging a tunnel parallel to the city wall:

For a considerable number of days the besieged did not discover [the Romans] carrying away the earth from the shaft; but when the heaps of earth became too high to be concealed from those inside the city, the commanders of the besieged garrison set to work vigorously digging a trench inside, parallel to the wall. . . . When the trench was made to the desired depth, they next placed in a row along the bottom of the trench nearest the wall a number of brazen vessels made very thin . . . [and] listened for the noise of the digging outside. Having marked the spot indicated by any of these brazen vessels, which were extraordinarily sensitive and vibrated to the sound outside, they began digging from within . . . so calculated as to exactly hit the enemy's tunnel.

This is a fine description of the use of countertunnels to intercept and disrupt a tunneling enemy's efforts. (It is also the first description of using acoustics to detect tunnels, a strategy that has become ever more sophisticated, although not necessarily more effective, over time.) The Persian Empire's siege of the Roman city of Dura-Europos in AD 256 led to another new development: when Persian militaries tunneling under the walls of the city hit a Roman countertunnel, they filled it with a poisonous gas made from pitch and sulfur to asphyxiate the soldiers inside—the first known use of gas warfare. The art of tunneling and countertunneling continued throughout the Middle Ages, with militaries constantly looking for ways to gain the upper hand. At the Siege of Château Gaillard (1203–04), the castle built by English King Richard the Lion-Hearted, French soldiers encountered three stout defensive walls. They eventually managed to break through because they found an unguarded toilet chute that emptied into a chapel inside the castle.

In the sixteenth century, when gunpowder was added to the tunneling battlefield, the results were literally explosive and increasingly lethal. European armies developed sophisticated techniques for planting barrels of gunpowder in concealed trenches in order to undermine or blow up enemy fortifications, also known as saps (hence the term "sapper" for engineers who did this kind of dangerous work). This technique reached a stupendous climax during the American Civil War at the Siege of Petersburg in July 1864, when Union troops surreptitiously dug a tunnel under

Confederate lines, only to fill it with so many barrels of gunpowder that they weren't able to climb out from the resulting crater. In what became known as the Battle of the Crater, Confederate soldiers simply lined up around the edge of the tunnel and poured down deadly fire on their helpless foes.

By the beginning of World War I, tunnel engineers' main task was no longer to build tunnels to fortify cities, but to build trenches on the western front. The trenches were essentially a static system of tunnels that served as front lines for each side; it wasn't long before militaries began building tunnels in order to try to blow up the trenches belonging to the enemy. The British proved the most adept at this. At the Battle of the Somme in 1916, they successfully exploded two enormous mines underneath the German trench. In 1917, at Messines Ridge, the British military devised an elaborate strategy to dig 22 separate tunnels or mine shafts underneath German lines over 18 months. The Germans discovered one of the shafts, which had to be abandoned, but the other 21 were finished undetected and stuffed with 450 tons of TNT. On May 30, shortly before the explosives were detonated, the British General Herbert Plumer told his staff, "Gentlemen, we may not make history tomorrow, but we shall certainly change the geography." The explosion ripped the entire crest off the Messines-Wytschaete Ridge with a blast so enormous that British Prime Minister David Lloyd George claimed to hear it at 10 Downing Street in London. Ten thousand German soldiers were instantly killed or entombed. Plumer, however, was right. Although the British took what was left of the Messines Ridge, the war didn't change course. Instead, it dragged on for another year and a half.

UNDERNEATH THE GOOD WAR

World War I brought three great innovations to the battlefield— the land tank, massed artillery firing high-explosive shells, and the airplane—that made armies feel increasingly vulnerable sitting out in the open. After the war, some military strategists responded by trying to put entire armies underground, in subterranean

complexes connected by tunnels to supposedly impregnable case-
ments and fortifications. The most famous (and the most futile) of
these efforts was France's so-called Maginot Line, an elaborate underground system of bunkers and supply depots supporting 22
large, aboveground forts and 36 smaller forts, all connected by a
railway, pulled by diesel-powered locomotives, that passed through
a network of tunnels. In 1940, however, Germany's mobile blitz-
krieg tactics completely bypassed the Maginot Line and France
had all but lost the war before the thousands of soldiers in the for-
tresses could even fire a shot.

The U.S. Army built something similar, but on a much smaller
scale, on the island of Corregidor in Manila Bay, with an
831-foot-long tunnel, some 24 feet wide and 18 feet high, feeding
ammunition and supplies to a complex of artillery positions chis-
eled out of solid rock. An additional 24 lateral tunnels provided
storage and sleeping quarters for troops. This was where U.S. General Douglas MacArthur, his family and staff, and Philippine President Manuel Quezon took refuge during the Japanese invasion of
the Philippine island of Luzon in December 1941. But like its Maginot Line counterpart, the Malinta Tunnel on Corregidor turned
out to be more of a trap than an impregnable fortress, as the new
mobile warfare techniques of World War II left it isolated and use-
less. Today, both are little more than tourist attractions and symbols of military folly.

But around the same time that these massive underground complexes were being built, tunnels also experienced a revival as a tool
for insurgents. The pioneers in this revival of tunnel warfare were
the Chinese during the Sino-Japanese War, especially during the
fighting around the village of Ranzhuang in Hebei Province in
1937 and 1938. Chinese guerrillas dug nine miles of tunnels between houses in the village to foxholes on the battlefield, so that
they could attack Japanese soldiers from the rear. The tunnel en-
trances and exits were usually located in a house or in a well, making it easier for guerrillas to enter and leave without being
detected.

The Japanese soon caught on, however, and began filling the tunnels with water or even poison gas. The Chinese retaliated by installing filtering systems that drew off the water and the gas. This cat-and-mouse game—which is typical of tunnel warfare—continued until the Japanese finally withdrew. How important the tunnels of Ranzhuang were to the battle's outcome is a matter of debate. To the Chinese, however, they are a monument to defiant resistance to the Japanese invader and, like the Maginot Line, are a major tourist attraction.

What the Japanese learned from the tunnel wars against the Chinese, however, would be invaluable in their fight against the U.S. Marines in World War II. They borrowed the techniques of hidden bunkers and emplacements connected by an elaborate network of tunnels, first on the island of Peleliu and then on Iwo Jima. There, they turned an entire mountain, Mount Suribachi, into a honeycomb of tunnels and bunkers lined with concrete, with multiple exits so that Marines clearing one end of the tunnels would find themselves suddenly under attack from the other end.

Clearing the Japanese tunnels was a grim business. Facing Japanese soldiers determined to fight to the death, U.S. Marines favored flamethrowers, explosive charges, and hand grenades (according to U.S. rules of engagement, poison gas was not an option). Marines on Peleliu suffered twice as many casualties as Marines fighting on Tarawa, largely because of the tunnels; the Marines on Iwo Jima were still clearing tunnels two months after the island had fallen.

There was method to the Japanese soldiers' madness. They hoped that by inflicting as many U.S. casualties as possible—and making the United States' path to victory as slow, painful, and costly as possible—they would deter Washington from attempting a similar full-scale invasion of Japan's home islands. It worked, but not in the way the Japanese had hoped. In order to avoid an invasion, U.S. President Harry Truman chose to end the war by dropping atomic bombs on the Japanese cities of Hiroshima and Nagasaki.

UNDERMINING THE UNITED STATES

The dawn of the atomic age forced militaries to dig even deeper underground to protect the chains of command from nuclear attack. So the United States built supposedly nuclear-bomb-proof shelters, including a five-acre network of tunnels buried under 2,000 feet of solid granite built into Cheyenne Mountain, Colorado, to house the North American Aerospace Defense Command; and the Presidential Emergency Operations Center, located 120 feet under the East Wing of the White House. Fortunately, neither one has been put to that ultimate test, although the PEOC was used by Vice President Dick Cheney during the 9/11 crisis.

But the most adept students of tunnel warfare during the Cold War were the Communist forces in the Korean and Vietnam conflicts. In Korea, underground warfare reached a new level of size and sophistication in the 1950s. To evade American air supremacy, North Korean and Chinese forces built underground fortifications so extensive that for every mile of military front on the surface, there were two miles of underground tunnels—more than 300 miles in total. The tunnels were built largely by prisoners, who ripped out more than two million cubic meters of rock for structures that hid not only tens of thousands of soldiers and supplies, but entire artillery batteries that could be wheeled out of mountain caves to fire on South Korean or UN forces (and then drawn back in to dodge subsequent airstrikes).

The tunnels dug by Communist forces in South Vietnam were nowhere near as massive as the North Korean version, but they enabled the Vietcong to maintain a guerrilla war for years against a more numerous and better-armed foe. The biggest underground complex was the tunnels at Cu Chi close to Saigon, initiated during Vietnam's Communist insurgency against the French colonial military in the 1950s. These tunnels extended some 200 miles toward the Cambodian border and came complete with ammunition storage, barracks, workshops, kitchens, hospitals, and even theaters for showing propaganda movies.

The U.S. military was so oblivious to the underground threat, at least at first, that in 1966 U.S. troops built a base camp—a 1,500-acre compound housing 4,500 troops—at Cu Chi, directly over the Vietcong tunnels. Black-clad guerrillas soon began organizing attacks on the base, popping out at night to blow up planes and steal weapons and equipment, including a tank, before disappearing into the darkness. The U.S. military responded by declaring the area around Cu Chi a "free fire" zone and pounded it with artillery, bombs, and even napalm in hopes of destroying the Vietcong. Yet the raids continued: from their tunnels, the Vietnamese guerrillas could wait out U.S. bombing raids and then prepare to strike again. The tunnels "were like a thorn stabbing the enemy in the eye," a Vietcong officer later remembered, one that had become impossible for the U.S. military to remove. According to one historian, the tunnels had allowed the Vietcong to so deeply infiltrate the U.S. military installation that at one point, all 13 of the base's barbers were members of the Vietcong.

When at last an Australian engineer revealed that the tunnels under the base were more extensive than anyone imagined, the U.S. Army realized what a hornets' nest it was sitting on. The effort to clear the tunnels included teams of Australians, Americans, and New Zealanders dubbed "Tunnel Rats" who entered small surface access holes barely two feet wide, usually armed with nothing more than a flashlight, a few grenades, and a small pistol. What they found was a vast labyrinth of communication tunnels leading to caves and caverns built at four separate levels. With nerve and courage, the Tunnel Rats defied the claustrophobic and cramped conditions—as well as booby traps, snakes, scorpions, hordes of bats, and angry Vietcong fighters—to clear the Cu Chi complex from the inside. At the same time, B-52 airstrikes pounded the tunnels from above, causing many to collapse. Some 12,000 Vietcong fighters were killed in the Cu Chi operation, but the United States had barely started securing the tunnel complex when the country withdrew from the war. Today, even the Vietnamese honor the Tunnel Rats as the toughest, deadliest foe they ever faced. (The

Israeli military has a similar unit, the Samoorim ["Weasels"], as part of the elite Yahalom combat engineers.) Although the Tunnel Rats could not save the U.S. mission in Vietnam, they did write one of the grittiest, if largely forgotten, chapters in the history of the U.S. Army.

In Vietnam, the tunnel digging stopped with the end of the war (although the Vietnamese revived their use during the Chinese invasion in 1978). Not so in North Korea. After the Korean War, Pyongyang's appetite for tunnels increased. In preparation for a fresh invasion of South Korea, North Korea designed tunnel complexes across the demilitarized zone between the two countries. Between 1974 and 1990, South Korean authorities discovered four massive tunnels extending from North Korea under the border, each buried more than 100 meters under the surface and measuring two meters high and two meters wide—wide enough for three North Korean soldiers to march through shoulder to shoulder (sufficient for a full division of North Korean troops, roughly 10,000 soldiers, to march through every hour). One of the tunnels emptied out just 30 miles from the South Korean capital of Seoul. South Korean authorities closed down the tunnels as they found them, but no one knows how many more may remain undiscovered.

THE INVISIBLE THREAT

The Israel Defense Forces face similar problems in Gaza today. In the IDF's recent incursion into Hamas-governed territory, it has claimed that it destroyed no fewer than 31 military tunnels leading into Israel. But there is no doubt that a large maze of tunnels still exists in Gaza.

These tunnels were clearly not the product of improvisation. Indeed, their size and sophistication suggest that, in recent years, North Korea has been providing Hamas both weapons and expertise in digging tunnels. The construction of Hamas' tunnels involved the removal of massive quantities of earth almost entirely with electric jackhammers operating some 60 feet underground, in order not to alert the Israelis. Then the surfaces of the tunnel were lined with concrete, and iron rails were installed down the middle to facilitate the transportation of soldiers, missiles, and weapons in—and kidnapped Israeli victims out. Some of Hamas' tunnels were large enough to drive a truck through, and nearly all were booby-trapped. They were also positioned so that detecting and clearing the tunnels would cause massive civilian casualties on the surface. Hamas' main underground command center, for example, is situated under a hospital.

What the IDF discovered, to its dismay, was that Hamas' tunnels weren't simply extensive—they were also jam-packed with weapons in preparation for an all-out offensive into Israel that Israeli authorities say was planned to coincide with the Rosh Hashanah holiday on September 24. If Hamas' rocket attacks hadn't triggered a bold Israeli reaction, including ground operations in Gaza, the tunnels might have gone undetected—and the coming Hamas offensive would have been as much a psychological blow to Israel as the 9/11 attacks were to the United States.

This is, of course, the great advantage of tunnels in warfare. They are an invisible and silent threat, unless you know what to look for and where to look. More often than not, countertunnelers have had to rely on luck, instinct, and human intelligence (that is to say, an informer) to find their whereabouts—and, as history has shown in Cu Chi and Messines Ridge, by the time they find out, it's often too late. Meanwhile, the factor of the unknown can gnaw at an antagonist's imagination, filling an entire community with fear and adding a dimension of psychological warfare to the other challenges tunnel warfare poses.

No one in Israel can be sure that the IDF has taken out all of the tunnels Hamas has built, any more than they know how many tunnels Hamas' Shiite counterpart, Hezbollah, has dug into Israel from Lebanon. Reports suggest that the Hezbollah tunnels may be, if anything, even more sophisticated. Likewise, South Koreans cannot be sure they've found every tunnel that their Communist neighbor has burrowed under the demilitarized zone, although no new tunnel has been found since 1991.

TECHNOLOGY VS. TUNNELS

Even the United States can't rest easy. The recent uncovering of more than 200 tunnels dug across the Mexican-U.S. border—95 in Nogales, Arizona, alone—has spurred fears of an underground assault. Most of these cross-border tunnels are used for smuggling illegal immigrants or drugs; but they could also become conduits for terrorists. That danger has prompted the Pentagon and the Department of Homeland Security (DHS) to develop new ways of detecting tunnels that are more systematic than relying on dumb luck or the occasional informant. In January 2011, the U.S. government even set up a Joint Tunnel Test Range at the Yuma Proving Ground in Yuma, Arizona, to sample the latest anti-tunneling technologies.

High-tech tunnel detection is an inexact science, to say the least. One underground detection expert, Paul Berman, has told the *Times of Israel* newspaper that electrical resistivity tomography, which measures levels of resistance in the earth under a given patch of ground, can find anomalies that would point to the existence of tunnels—or again might not. So far, no one has found the magic high-tech formula for finding hidden tunnels. "Tunnels have only been, so far, successfully located by intelligence, not by technology," according to John Verrico of the DHS Science and Technology Directorate. Seismic testing technologies that help oil and gas exploration or the construction trade find the geophysical character of a piece of land aren't designed to look for the distinctive features of tunnels. Sensors that work well in finding gaps or crevasses in one environment may miss significant features of another, including the presence of a man-made tunnel.

Ground-penetrating radar has been one promising area of research, using pulses of radio frequency energy to find voids or gaps beneath ground surface. GPR works fine for locating utility lines and minesweeping operations and finding buried historical sites.

But looking deeper, to the 10- to 20-meter depths where terrorists like to lay their tunnels, is more difficult. Lockheed Martin is working with the DHS on a lower-frequency version of GPR, using electromagnetic waves to plot tunnels deep underground, but until now the results have been indeterminate.

Another promising approach is the prototype Active Acoustic Tunnel Detector, being developed at Idaho National Laboratory, which transmits up to 200 hertz of acoustic waves into the ground. An onboard motion detector measures how the waves move the dirt and rock that those sound waves pass through. If the ground is solid, the resulting graph shows a rapidly rising line. If there's a gap or void, the graph line will appear as a hump or dip. A third approach uses microgravity analysis, measuring minute changes in the planet's gravitational field to locate a tunnel. That requires a higher level of precision than current testing can show and will require a heavy investment in research to get any reliable results.

In any case, once a tunnel is found, there still remains the problem of how to clear or secure it safely, especially if it's booby-trapped. The use of robotic vehicles to explore and neutralize a tunnel structure may eventually replace the volunteer "Tunnel Rat." But for now, the old techniques of clearing them with explosives and a handgun remain the standard—as do the dangers of that approach.

In fact, if there's any certain bet to come out of the fighting in Gaza, it's that tunnel warfare in the hands of future insurgencies and militant groups will pose a persistent problem in spite of all the high-tech weaponry and gadgets of traditional militaries. Which side ultimately prevails depends on many factors. But anyone who thinks there's clear light at the end of this tunnel had better think again.

ARTHUR HERMAN is a Senior Fellow at the Hudson Institute and author of *Freedom's Forge: How American Business Produced Victory in World War II.* Follow him on Twitter @ArthurLHerman.

Golden Rule

Why Beijing Is Buying

By Alan Greenspan   SEPTEMBER 29, 2014

A sales representative poses behind a 24K gold dragon, December 6, 2011.
(Bobby Yip / Courtesy Reuters)

If China were to convert a relatively modest part of its $4 tril-
lion foreign exchange reserves into gold, the country's currency
could take on unexpected strength in today's international financial system. It would be a gamble, of course, for China to use
part of its reserves to buy enough gold bullion to displace the
United States from its position as the world's largest holder of
monetary gold. (As of spring 2014, U.S. holdings amounted to
$328 billion.) But the penalty for being wrong, in terms of lost
interest and the cost of storage, would be modest. For the rest
of the world, gold prices would certainly rise, but only during

the period of accumulation. They would likely fall back once China reached its goal.

The broader issue—a return to the gold standard in any form—is nowhere on anybody's horizon. It has few supporters in today's virtually universal embrace of fiat currencies and floating exchange rates. Yet gold has special properties that no other currency, with the possible exception of silver, can claim. For more than two millennia, gold has had virtually unquestioned acceptance as payment. It has never required the credit guarantee of a third party. No questions are raised when gold or direct claims to gold are offered in payment of an obligation; it was the only form of payment, for example, that exporters to Germany would accept as World War II was drawing to a close. Today, the acceptance of fiat money—currency not backed by an asset of intrinsic value—rests on the credit guarantee of sovereign nations endowed with effective taxing power, a guarantee that in crisis conditions has not always matched the universal acceptability of gold.

If the dollar or any other fiat currency were universally acceptable at all times, central banks would see no need to hold any gold. The fact that they do indicates that such currencies are not a universal substitute. Of the 30 advanced countries that report to the International Monetary Fund, only four hold no gold as part of their reserve balances. Indeed, at market prices, the gold held by the central banks of developed economies was worth $762 billion as of December 31, 2013, comprising 10.3 percent of their overall reserve balances. (The IMF held an additional $117 billion.) If, in the words of the British economist John Maynard Keynes, gold were a "barbarous relic," central banks around the world would not have so much of an asset whose rate of return, including storage costs, is negative.

There have been several cases where policymakers have contemplated selling off gold bullion. In 1976, for example, I participated, as chair of the Council of Economic Advisers, in a conversation in which then U.S. Treasury Secretary William Simon and then Federal Reserve Board Chair Arthur Burns met with President Gerald

Ford to discuss Simon's recommendation that the United States sell its 275 million ounces of gold and invest the proceeds in interest-earning assets. Whereas Simon, following the economist Milton Friedman's view at that time, argued that gold no longer served any useful monetary purpose, Burns argued that gold was the ultimate crisis backstop to the dollar. The two advocates were unable to find common ground. In the end, Ford chose to do nothing. And to this day, the U.S. gold hoard has changed little, amounting to 261 million ounces.

I confronted the issue again as Fed chair in the 1990s, following a decline in the price of gold to under $300 an ounce. One of the periodic meetings of the G-10 governors was dedicated to the issue of the European members' desire to pare their gold holdings. But they were aware that in competing with each other to sell, they could drive the price of gold down still further. They all agreed to an allocation arrangement of who would sell how much and when. Washington abstained. The arrangement was renewed in 2014. In a statement accompanying the announcement, the European Central Bank simply stated, "Gold remains an important element of global monetary reserves."

Beijing, meanwhile, clearly has no ideological aversion to keeping gold. From 1980 to the end of 2002, Chinese authorities held on to nearly 13 million ounces. They boosted their holdings to 19 million ounces in December 2002, and to 34 million ounces in April 2009. At the end of 2013, China was the world's fifth-largest sovereign holder of gold, behind only the United States (261 million ounces), Germany (109 million ounces), Italy (79 million ounces), and France (78 million ounces). The IMF had 90 million ounces.

However much gold China accumulates, though, a larger issue remains unresolved: whether free, unregulated capital markets can coexist with an authoritarian state. China has progressed a long way from the early initiatives of Chinese leader Deng Xiaoping. It is approaching the unthinkable goal of matching the United States in total GDP, even if only in terms of purchasing-power parity. But going forward, the large gains of recent years are going to become ever more difficult to sustain.

It thus seems unlikely that, in the years immediately ahead, China is going to be successful in vaulting over the United States technologically, more for political than economic reasons. A culture that is politically highly conformist leaves little room for unorthodox thinking. By definition, innovation requires stepping outside the bounds of conventional wisdom, which is always difficult in a society that inhibits freedom of speech and action.

To date, Beijing has been able to maintain a viable and largely politically stable society mainly because the political restraints of a one-party state have been offset by the degree to which the state is seen to provide economic growth and material wellbeing. But in the years ahead, that is less likely to be the case, as China's growth rates slow and its competitive advantage narrows.

ALAN GREENSPAN served as Chair of the U.S. Federal Reserve from 1987 to 2006. This essay is adapted from the paperback edition of his most recent book, The Map and the Territory: Risk, Human Nature, and the Future of Forecasting (Penguin Press, 2014). Copyright © Alan Greenspan, 2014. Reprinted by arrangement with the Penguin Press.

The Poor and the Sick

What Cholera and Ebola Have in Common

Fran Quigley   OCTOBER 19, 2014

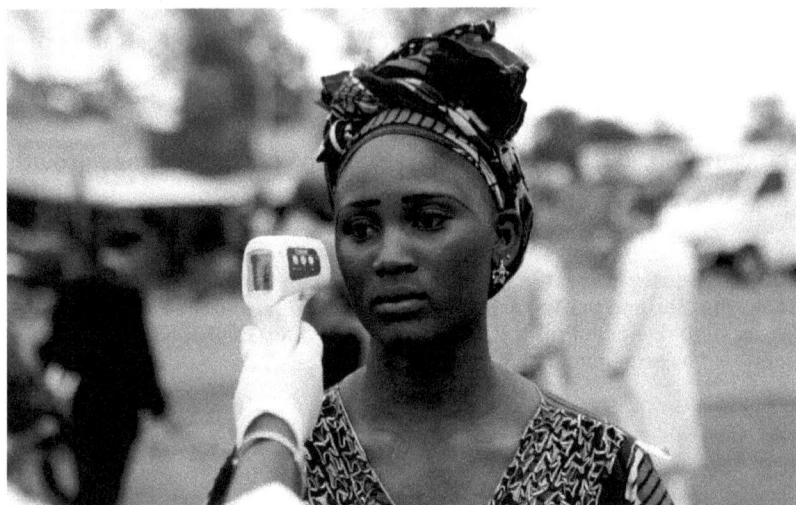

A health worker checks the temperature of a woman entering Mali from Guinea at the border in Kouremale, October 2, 2014. (Joe Penney / Courtesy Reuters)

The two deadliest outbreaks of this century can be traced to one thing: poverty. Cholera exploded in the Haitian countryside in October 2010, infecting more than 600,000 people and killing 8,600. Ebola surfaced this March in Guinea and has since spread to Liberia and Sierra Leone. As of mid-October, more than 8,000 have been infected and 4,000 have died, almost exclusively in West Africa.

At first glance, the two outbreaks couldn't be less similar. Cholera moves quickly but it is a nineteenth-century disease, easily thwarted by modern water treatment systems and health care. It ravaged Haiti, but it has not spread beyond the developing world. Ebola, on the other hand, moves slowly and is not as easily treated. Further, it has reached the United States, earning it near-obsessive attention in U.S. news. As Greg Gonsalves, co-director of the Yale Global Health Justice Partnership wrote this month in Quartz, "Exotic infections for Americans, often from far away places, often Africa, strike fear into their hearts, but only once the pathogens have cleared customs." Ebola has cleared customs in a way Haitian cholera never has.

But a look at the long list of casualties reveals what the two diseases have in common. The right to health comes with a cover charge, and much of the world—especially those in struggling states such as Haiti, Liberia, and Sierra Leone—can't pay it. In Haiti, cholera found its ideal host. The poorest country in the Western Hemisphere, Haiti lacks any system of modern water treatment. In the fall of 2010, United Nations peacekeeping troops from Nepal imported cholera to Haiti. They were stationed at a military base in rural Haiti, where their sewage was dumped, untreated, into Haiti's waterways. As Paul S. Keim, a geneticist who studied the Haitian and Nepalese cholera strains, told *The New York Times*, in 2012, "It was like throwing a lighted match into a gasoline-filled room."

Ebola arrived in similarly combustible terrain in West Africa. Violent conflicts in Liberia had left only 51 doctors to care for more than four million people. The country runs a deficit in medicine, supplies, facilities, and trained nurses and doctors. Guinea and Sierra Leone face similar constraints.

To understand the impact these conditions had on the scale of the outbreak, consider a counterfactual: What would have happened had the outbreaks first surfaced in my hometown, Indianapolis, Indiana, instead of Haiti or West Africa? For one thing, it's unlikely that cholera would have infected anyone at all. Rigorously enforced public health laws would have prevented filthy sewage disposal practices, and even if they hadn't, effective sewage treatment would have eradicated the bacteria before it entered the drinking water. If anyone did somehow become infected, any emergency room would be prepared to offer the fluids and antibiotics that, when provided promptly, eliminate the infection in over 99 percent of cases.

As for Ebola, we know how the United States would respond. Those suspected of being infected would be isolated and provided care in a way that also protects health-care workers. All the while, at the state and federal levels, officials would implement a public health communication and response strategy. That two Dallas health-care workers were infected is worrisome, of course, but there is every reason to believe they will remain an anomaly. And the two cases pale in comparison to the 8,000 victims in West Africa, a number that is likely to keep growing. As Jim Yong Kim, president of the World Bank, and Paul Farmer, a professor at Harvard, wrote in an August op-ed in The Washington Post, "A functioning health system can stop Ebola transmission."

Yet functioning health systems have proved elusive for the world's poor—even though the right to health is codified in the Universal Declaration of Human Rights. And it is difficult to get richer countries to fight massive outbreaks that have not yet reached their borders. Diseases such as Ebola, which affect primarily the global poor, are unattractive targets for pharmaceutical companies looking to maximize profit. Government-funded research has its own budget limitations. According to Dr. Francis Collins, the director of the U.S. National Institutes of Health, an Ebola vaccine would already exist had the U.S. government not slashed research funding.

Public health experts have been quick to point out that poverty— and the accompanying lack of health-care access—is something far more likely to be endured by people of color. The United Nations has refused to admit its role in spreading cholera in Haiti, or to offer any reparations, a response that seems unthinkable had the outbreak occurred in Europe or the United States. In an interview with Public Radio International, Joia Mukherjee, a professor at Harvard Medical School and chief medical officer at the

Boston-based nonprofit Partners in Health, blamed racism for the slow international response to the Ebola crisis. "I think it's easy for the world—the powerful world, who are largely non-African, non–people of color—to ignore the suffering of poor black people." The gold standard of care provided to white Americans and Europeans infected by Ebola, compared to the substandard treatment of West Africans, bears out her point.

Of course, Ebola's arrival in the United States has already changed the international response to the outbreak. Efforts to create a vaccine have been fast-tracked, and nonprofits have launched community-based programs in West Africa to combat Ebola and other less sensational killers such as malaria and infectious diarrhea.

But if the cholera outbreak serves as any indication, West Africans should not be too optimistic. This week marks four years since cholera surfaced in Haiti, and the anniversary will pass with no reparations for affected Haitians, no new water treatment system to prevent future outbreaks, and no guarantee that the disease will stop claiming victims. If Ebola is to be any different, the response must target the root of the problem: the deep-seated poverty that has allowed it to spread.

FRAN QUIGLEY is Clinical Professor and Director of the Health and Human Rights Clinic at Indiana University McKinney School of Law and is the author of How Human Rights Can Build Haiti.

The Myth of the Caliphate

The Political History of an Idea

Nick Danforth   NOVEMBER 19, 2014

Abdulhamid II, who would become one of the last Ottoman sultans and caliphs, as a prince in 1867. (W.&D. DOWNEY / Jebulon)

In 1924, Turkish leader Kemal Ataturk officially abolished the Ottoman caliphate. Today, most Western discussions of the Islamic State of Iraq and al-Sham (ISIS), the extremist group that has declared a caliphate across much of Iraq and Syria, begin by referencing this event as if it were a profound turning point in Islamic history. Some contemporary Islamists think of it this way, too: there's a reason, for example, that *Lion Cub,* the Muslim Brotherhood's children's publication, once awarded the "Jewish" "traitor" Ataturk multiple first prizes in its "Know the Enemies of Your Religion" contest.

Even if today's Islamists reference the Ottomans, though, most of them are much more focused on trying to re-create earlier caliphates: the era of the four Rightly Guided Caliphs, who ruled immediately after Muhammad's death in the seventh century, for example, or the Abbasid caliphate, which existed in one form or another from the ninth to the thirteenth centuries (before being officially abolished by the Mongols). By conflating the nineteenth-century Ottoman royal family with these caliphs from a millennium ago or more, Western pundits and nostalgic Muslim thinkers alike have built up a narrative of the caliphate as an enduring institution, central to Islam and Islamic thought between the seventh and twentieth centuries. In fact, the caliphate is a political or religious idea whose relevance has waxed and waned according to circumstance.

The caliphate's more recent history under the Ottomans shows why the institution might be better thought of as a political fantasy—a blank slate just as nebulous as the "dictatorship of the proletariat"—that contemporary Islamists are largely making up as they go along. (If it weren't, ISIS could not so readily use the same term to describe their rogue and bloody statelet that Muslim British businessmen use to articulate the idea of an elected and democratic leader for the Islamic world.) What's more, the story of the Ottoman caliphate also suggests that in trying to realize almost any version of this fantasy, contemporary Islamists may well confront the same contradictions that bedeviled the Ottomans a century ago.

OTTOMAN REBRANDING

When the Ottoman Empire conquered Egypt and the Arabian Peninsula in 1517, Sultan Selim the Grim officially claimed the title of caliph for himself and his heirs. In addition to taking control of the cities of Mecca and Medina, Selim bolstered his claim by bringing a collection of the Prophet's garments and beard hairs back to Istanbul.

Centuries after the fact, the Ottomans decided that they needed to make the whole process look a little more respectable, so royal historians began to assert that the final heir to the Abbasid caliphate, living in exile in Cairo centuries after losing his throne, had voluntarily bestowed his title on Selim. More practically, the Ottomans buttressed their claim to Islamic leadership by serving as guardians of the hajj and sending an elaborately decorated gilt mantle to cover the Kaaba each year.

To put the title grab in perspective, when the Ottoman Sultan Mehmed II conquered the Byzantine capital of Constantinople 64 years before Selim conquered Egypt, he had claimed the title Caesar of Rome for his descendants. To the extent that being caliph had any more purchase than being Caesar for the Ottomans in the late nineteenth century, it was largely the result of a political campaign on the part of Sultan Abdulhamid II to rally anticolonial sentiment around the Ottoman state and to boost his own domestic legitimacy. His techniques included seeking to have his name read out at Friday prayers and distributing Korans around the Muslim world from Africa to Indonesia.

There is no doubt that many Muslims, faced with the triumph of European colonialism in their own countries, did come to admire the idea of a pious and powerful leader like the Ottoman sultan defying Western imperialism on behalf of the entire Muslim world. Certainly, British and French officials expressed increasing fear about his potential power over Muslim colonial subjects in North Africa and India. Although he was eager to try to leverage such fears, however, even Abdulhamid had his misgivings about how much real influence his efforts won him in such far-flung locales.

One thing that particularly worried him was the fact that not everyone accepted his claims on the caliphate. Separate from those who rallied around Abdulhamid out of religious solidarity were others, motived by Arab nationalism or dissatisfaction with Abdulhamid's tyranny, who questioned the religious foundation of his rule. Such thinkers, including at some points Rashid Rida, justified the creation of a different, Arab caliphate by quoting Muhammad as saying that the true caliph needed to be a descendant of the Prophet's Quraysh tribe. (The Ottomans, it seems, accepted the validity of this quote but had their own interpretation of it, in which the Prophet actually meant that the caliph didn't need to be a descendant of the Quraysh tribe.)

But in either case, the violent politics of the early twentieth century quickly outmatched theology. Despite his best efforts as defender of the faith, Abdulhamid kept losing territory and political power to Christian imperialist forces. That helped the secular leaders of the Young Turk movement, such as Enver Pasha, sideline the sultan and take power for themselves on the eve of World War I. When the Ottoman Empire then enjoyed some military success, belatedly holding its own in the Second Balkan War, Enver became an inspiration to the Muslim world. Indeed, the list of babies reportedly named after him at the time includes Enver Hoxha, the future leader of Albania, and Anwar al-Sadat, the future leader of Egypt.

ARAB HEIR

Of course, Enver's own star faded, too, with the Ottoman defeat at the end of World War I. Ataturk quickly emerged as a new hero by leading a successful campaign to drive French, Italian, British, and Greek armies out of Ottoman Anatolia. Quickly, some of the same politically attuned Muslims who had supported Abdulhamid's anti-imperial caliphate found even more to admire in Ataturk's armed defiance of European might. In Palestine, for example, Muslims who had once turned to the Ottoman caliph for protection against Zionist settlers and British occupiers began to cheer Ataturk, leading one suspicious British officer to worry that the Turkish figure had become "a new savior of Islam."

At the same time, the decline of Ottoman power before, during, and after World War I loaned increasing credence to the idea of a new, non-Ottoman caliph in the Arab world. But it was never entirely clear just who that Arab caliph would be. The result was that when Ataturk finally abolished the institution of the caliphate in 1924, there was no clear or coherent outcry from the Muslim world as a whole. Many Muslims, particularly those in India for whom pan-Islamic symbols such as the caliph were an important part of anticolonialism, protested. Others were more interested in maneuvering to claim the title for themselves.

Most famous was Husayn ibn Ali, sherif of Mecca, who is known to Lawrence of Arabia fans for his leading role in the Arab Revolt. As the local leader with control of Mecca and Medina—and a supposedly clear line of descent from the Prophet's tribe—Husayn believed that after driving the Ottomans out of the Middle East, he could become an Arab king, with all the religious and temporal powers of the caliph. In pursuit of this goal, when Ataturk exiled the Ottoman sultan, Husayn invited him to Mecca. (The exiled monarch soon decided he preferred the Italian Riviera.)

Several years later, Husayn's son Abdullah—founder of the Jordanian monarchy—would declare that, in ending the caliphate, Turks had "rendered the greatest possible service to the Arabs," for which he felt like "sending a telegram thanking Mustafa Kemal." Of course, Husayn's plans didn't come off exactly as expected. Despite getting British backing for his scheme early in the war, he famously fell afoul of the Sykes-Picot Agreement. The French drove his son out of Syria, and before long, the Saudis drove him out of the Arabian Peninsula. By the time Husayn officially declared himself caliph, supposedly at the insistence of a select group of Muslim leaders, his power had dwindled to the point where the declaration seemed like an act of pure desperation.

The Egyptian monarchy, meanwhile, had a claim of its own to advance. Despite being closely aligned with the British and descended from Circassian Albanian ancestors with no tie to the Prophet's family, King Fuad covertly put forward his case to succeed the Ottomans. In the words of one Islamic scholar, Egypt was better suited to the caliphate than, say, a desert nomad like Husayn "because she took the lead in religious education and had a vast number of highly educated and intelligent Muslims." King Idris I of Libya also seemed to consider making a bid for the title but, like Fuad, ultimately decided he had too little support to do so officially.

Saudi Arabia's King Saud, despite eventually seizing the Holy Land from Husayn, was one of the few leaders who never put forward a claim to the caliphate, although the idea was certainly discussed. Saud was aligned with the Wahhabi movement, which arose as a rebellion against the supposed decadence of the Ottoman government in the eighteenth century. Ironically, although his opposition to the Ottoman-style caliph was shared by other Arabs, his particular brand of religiosity was too radical for him to ever think he had much chance of becoming caliph himself.

In the end, though, the unseemliness of such political wrangling was just one of the factors that helped put the caliphate discussion to rest for the next several decades. Many Muslims had responded to its abolition by redoubling their efforts to build secular constitutional governments in their own countries. Indeed, some of the strongest opposition to the Egyptian king's caliphal aspirations came from Egyptian liberals who opposed any moves that would increase the monarchy's power. Egyptian scholar Ali Abd al-Raziq, in his famously controversial criticism of the very idea of a caliphate, even went so far as to claim that the Koran contains "no reference to the caliphate that Muslims have been calling for." This was also the period where a number of thinkers, secularists and religious Muslims alike, began discussing the possibility that the caliph should be a purely religious figure, like an "Islamic pope," unencumbered by any temporal power.

A HOPE AND A PRAYER

It would be a mistake to think that twenty-first-century Islamist movements trying to revive the caliphate are doing so in the name of a clear, well-defined Islamic mandate. Rather, they are just other players in a centuries-long debate about a concept that has only occasionally taken on widespread relevance in the Islamic world.

The legacy of earlier rounds of this argument can still be felt today. It is no surprise that, as a historical inspiration, the Ottoman caliphate holds most sway among Turkish Islamists, whose nostalgia owes far more to the way Turkish nationalists have glorified the empire than it does to the piety of the sultans. Conversely, the religious legacy of Abd al-Wahhab's eighteenth-century critique of the Ottoman state, combined with the political legacy of more recent anti-Ottoman Arab nationalism, gives plenty of non-Turkish Islamists ample reason to prefer the precedent of an Arab caliphate.

By treating the Ottoman caliphate as the final historical reference point for what current Islamists aspire to, Western pundits conflate the contemporary dream of a powerful, universally respected Muslim leader with the late Ottoman sultan's failed dream of becoming such a figure himself. The circumstances uniting these dreams—and the appeal of strong religious power in the face of Western political, military, and economic power—may be the same. But so are the challenges. Contemporary claimants to the title of caliph may quickly find themselves in the same boat as Ottoman caliphs. Political or military success, rather than history or theology, can bring short-lived legitimacy, but failure in these realms will bring other contenders for power.

NICK DANFORTH is a doctoral candidate in Turkish history at Georgetown University.

www.ingramcontent.com/pod-product-compliance
Lightning Source LLC
Chambersburg PA
CBHW062219270326
41930CB00009B/1787